250 Tasty Quiche Recipes

(250 Tasty Quiche Recipes - Volume 1)

Mary Yoder

Content

250 Awesome Quiche Recipes

***

1. 3 Cheese Sausage Quiche Recipe

Serving: 6 | Prep: | Cook: 70mins | Ready in:

Ingredients

- 2 lb turkey sausage
- 1 med onion, diced
- 1 med bell pepper diced
- 1 tsp grated garlic
- 1 package fresh button mushrooms, chopped
- 1 sm head broccoli florettes only (optional)
- 1 c fresh spinich (optional)
- 2 c grated sharp cheddar cheese
- 1 c grated motzarella cheese
- 1 c grated provolone cheese
- 1 doz eggs, beaten
- 3 deep dish pie crust , bought or homemade

Direction

- Prick pie crusts with fork.
- Place in 375 F oven till slightly brown.
- Put on cabinet to cool.
- Brown meat in skillet.
- Add pepper, onion and garlic and cook till onions are clear.
- Mix together in large mixing bowl all other veggies, cheeses and eggs.
- Cool meat mixture before adding other ingredients.
- Incorporate all ingredients together and make sure is mixed well.
- Place ingredients into cooked pie shells-you can mound it some.
- Bake in 375F oven until uniformly brown.
- FREEZES BEAUTIFULLY!

2. ASPARAGUS HAM QUICHE Recipe

Serving: 12 | Prep: | Cook: 35mins | Ready in:

Ingredients

- Ingredients:
- 2 packages (10-oz each) frozen cut asparagus, thawed
- 1 pound fully cooked ham, chopped
- 2 cups (8-oz) shredded swiss cheese reduced-fat
- ½ cup chopped onion
- 6 eggs
- 2 cups 1% milk
- 1 ½ cups buttermilk baking mix
- 1 Tbs. dried parsley flakes
- ¼ tsp. pepper

Direction

- Preheat oven at 375.
- In two greased 9-inch pie plates, layer the asparagus, ham, cheese and onion. In a bowl, beat eggs. Add remaining ingredients and mix well. Divide mixture in half and pour over asparagus mixture in each pie plate. Bake at 375 for 30 minutes or until a knife inserted near the center comes out clean. Yield: 12 servings.
- Serving size: 1 slice
- Nutritional Values: Calories per serving: 261, Fat: 10g, Cholesterol: 148mg, Sodium: 687mg, Carbohydrate: 15g, Fiber: 1g, Protein: 18g

3. Almond Chicken Quiche Recipe

Serving: 8 | Prep: | Cook: 50mins | Ready in:

Ingredients

- 5 eggs
- 1 ½ c Half and Half
- 6 oz small diced cooked chicken
- 4 oz gruyere cheese, shredded
- 4 oz thinly sliced mushrooms
- 2 oz parmesan cheese, grated
- 1 oz toasted blanched almonds
- 1-2 T finely sliced green onions
- 1 T unsalted butter
- ½ t salt
- ¼ t white pepper
- Fresh ground nutmeg to taste
- 1 deep dish 9 inch pie shell ~ 6 cups

Direction

- Preheat oven to 400*F.
- Blind bake docked pie shell for 10 minutes, remove weights and cook for 3 minutes more or until you have a lightly browned crust. Remove from oven and cool a couple of minutes.
- Sauté the mushrooms and green onions in butter until wilted and water has evaporated.
- Place the mushroom mixture on the bottom of the baked pie shell.
- Add the diced chicken to the dish.
- In a large bowl, whisk together the eggs, half and half do not foam the mixture.
- Add seasonings and cheeses mix well.
- Pour custard into the pie shell.
- Top with toasted almonds.
- Bake for 10 minutes then turn heat down to 350*F for 30 – 40 minutes longer or until the crust is golden and the filling is fully set.
- Allow 10 minutes cooling before cutting, serve warm or at room temperature.

4. Amandas Vegetable Quiche Recipe

Serving: 12 | Prep: | Cook: 45mins | Ready in:

Ingredients

- crust for 2 - 9 inch pies
- 13 eggs (room temp)
- 1 cup milk (room temp)
- 2 tsp salt
- pepper to taste
- 1 Tb Lea & Perrins worcestershire sauce
- 5 oz (1/2 pkg) bacon (cooked and diced)
- 1 small/medium bunch of broccoli (steamed 5 minutes - still slightly firm) coarsely chopped
- 1 onion (chopped and caramelized)
- 1 -2 cups of spinach (slightly wilted in skillet)
- 1/4 cup of Italian parsley
- 3 cups shredded cheese (any kind desired)
- Crust -
- 1 3/4 cup flour
- 6 Tb cold butter cut into small pieces
- 5 Tb cold shortening
- 1/2 tsp salt
- 2 Tb ice water

Direction

- Mix flour and salt. Cut butter and shortening into flour mixture until resembles coarse meal. Add water and knead. (If too dry add more water 1 tsp. at a time) Make into disc, put in plastic wrap and chill in refrigerator.
- Preheat oven to 350 deg.
- Roll out chilled crust to fit 9 x 13 dish (bottom and sides of dish buttered). Chill crust in freezer 10 minutes (remove from oven a few minutes before putting in oven so glass will warm up and not break in oven). Pre-bake crust 10 minutes. Remove from oven and cool.
- Filling -
- Caramelize onions; cook bacon and dice; steam broccoli 5 minutes and coarsely chop (broccoli should be still slightly firm); chop Italian parsley; slightly wilt spinach; shred cheese - can be done in advance.

- Preheat oven to 375 degrees.
- In a large bowl mix eggs, milk, salt, pepper and Worcestershire Sauce.
- Put 1/3 of cheese on top of crust. Add vegetable/meat mixture. Top with 1/3 of cheese. Pour egg mixture over vegetables, meat and cheese. Top with last 1/3 of cheese.
- Cook for 35 - 45 minutes or until firm. (Do not overcook or it will be dry)

5. Apple Sausage Cheddar Quiche Recipe

Serving: 8 | Prep: | Cook: 40mins | Ready in:

Ingredients

- 2 cups day old French bread
- 3 link sausages precooked and cut in 1/4" slices
- 1 granny smith apple peeled and chopped
- 3 eggs
- 1 cup milk
- 1-1/2 cups shredded cheddar cheese
- 1/4 cup shredded swiss cheese

Direction

- Tear bread into 1" inch pieces then cover bottom of quiche dish with bread pieces.
- Add sausage and apple then whisk eggs and milk together and pour over bread mixture.
- Bake at 350 for 40 minutes then cool 10 minutes before slicing.

6. Apple Bacon Quiche Recipe

Serving: 24 | Prep: | Cook: 30mins | Ready in:

Ingredients

- **Note for the first 4 ingredients, they can be skipped if using a premade pie dough.

- 2 ¼ cup Sifted flour
- 1 ½ tsp salt
- ¾ cup shortening
- 5 tbl Cold milk
- ***In lieu of the homemade pie crust use 2 premade pie crusts
- 5 eggs
- 1 tbl butter or margarine
- 1 cup Diced Canadian bacon or any good smoked bacon diced
- 2 cups Thinly sliced apples (red Delicious are good) (unpeeled) Don't use Granny smith or any tart apple, the flavor is not right with the saltiness of the swiss or the smokiness of the bacon or nutmeg
- 1 tbl flour
- 1 ¾ cup Half and half
- ⅛ tsp nutmeg
- ¼ tsp caraway seeds
- ½ tsp dry mustard
- 1 cup Shredded swiss cheese
- or 2 premade pie crusts

Direction

- ***For homemade pie crust
- Combine sifted flour and 1 teaspoon salt.
- Cut in shortening until particles are size of peas.
- Sprinkle with about 5 tablespoons cold milk, adding just enough to make stiff dough.
- Shape into 6 balls.
- Roll out on lightly floured board to 6-inch circles and fit into 6 (5-inch) tart pans.
- Fold edges under and build up high fluted rim.
- Continue to next section
- **If using ready-made pie crust continue from here
- Shape into 6 balls.
- Roll out pie crust on lightly floured board to 6-inch circles and fit into 6 (5-inch) tart pans.
- Pierce all over with fork tines.
- Separate 1 egg.
- Beat egg white lightly and brush over bottoms and sides of shells.
- Bake below centre of oven at 425F 15 minutes.

- Meanwhile, melt butter and sauté bacon 1 minute.
- Add apple slices, cover and cook about 10 minutes, until apples are almost translucent.
- Beat remaining whole eggs with remaining egg yolk.
- Add flour, half and half, remaining 1/2 teaspoon salt, nutmeg, caraway seeds and dry mustard and mix well.
- Sprinkle cheese evenly among tart shells, top with apples and bacon.
- Pour egg mixture into shells.
- Bake at 375F about 30 minutes, or until set in centre.
- Cool to lukewarm before cutting

7. Artechoke And Spinach Quiche Recipe

Serving: 68 | Prep: | Cook: 52mins | Ready in:

Ingredients

- 4- shallots or 1/4 cup red onion
- 1/2 red bell pepper diced
- i can artichoke hearts drained halves or pieces
- 1 bag- fresh spinach
- 4oz-8oz gruyere cheese grated, i use 4
- 8-eggs
- half and half 1-cup
- puff pastry
- nutmeg
- salt and pepper

Direction

- Sauté shallots and red bell pepper in 1 tbsp. evoo about 4 minutes add spinach until wilted about 2 minutes. Let cool.
- In bowl whisk 8 eggs add 1 cup half and half and pinch fresh nutmeg sea salt and pepper.
- In pie dish layer puff pastry in buttered dish fine if it hangs over.
- On top of shell pour in artichokes then add shallots and red bell pepper pour egg mixture

over it and sprinkle all over top with gruyere shredded cheese.
- Bake in preheated oven 350, bake until light golden brown around 50-55 minutes.

8. Artisian Asparagus Quiche Recipe

Serving: 6 | Prep: | Cook: 35mins | Ready in:

Ingredients

- 1 bunch of fresh baby asparagus (you'll need about 18 stalks depending upon size)
- 1/3 cup: chopped scallions (2 or 3 stalks) or 1/3 cup fresh sliced chives
- 4 slightly beaten eggs
- 1-1/2 tablespoons flour
- 1-1/2 cups of half-n-half, light cream or milk
- 1/2 box of frozen spinach - drained really well of its water and thawed
- 1 cup shredded cheese, use a combination of two or more cheeses such as goat, swiss and gouda or swiss, cheddar and monteray jack for some pizazz.
- 1 pie crust (pre-made ok to use...so it's ok to cheat on this step my peeps)
- 1/2 teaspoon salt
- 1/4 teaspoon fresh cracked pepper
- 1/8 teaspoon garlic powder
- 1/8 teaspoon of nutmeg (preferably fresh if possible)
- *****for homemade rustic pastry shell:
- 1 cup flour
- 1/2 teaspoon salt
- 1/3 cup chilled shortening
- 3 tablespoons butter
- 3 tablespoons freshly grated parmasean cheese
- Equipment Needed: One working oven at 450 to start, fresh chicken eggs just laid (just kidding), bag of dried beans out of their plastic, tin foil to help with baking pie shell blind (not you but the pie shell of course), steamer for asparagus, couple of bowls to

make work easier and a cookie sheet to make clean up easier by placing cookie sheet under pastry shell when baking quiche in avoiding any spills that may occur.

Direction

- To make rustic pie pastry:
- Place flour and shortening in food processor and pulse five times, add chilled water and pulse several more times creating pastry dough.
- No need to roll out, simply press pastry dough into pie pan - like you would when making shortening bread. One bottom is "filled" continue pushing up sides of pastry pan. Great to have kids help you on this part.
- Preheat oven at 450 degrees and take pre-made (or just made) pastry shell, and prick bottom with fork all over. Either use blind cooking method (bag of dried beans inside tin foil and place inside pastry shell to help prevent pastry shell from puffing up on bottom) or take empty pie shell and place on top of pastry shell.
- Bake pie shell for 5 minutes till pastry shell is set slightly.
- Take out of oven and let cool.
- If you have a steamer, steam asparagus for five minutes - keep them whole at this point - or blanch them in boiling water for three minutes then place in cold water bath to stop cooking. Reserve up to twelve pieces whole and chop up rest to have up to one cup of chopped asparagus.
- Take shredded cheese into a bowl and stir in flour, salt, pepper and garlic powder, stir till well incorporated.
- In other bowl, place eggs and whisk. Add half-n-half, chopped asparagus, chopped thawed out spinach, chopped scallions and shredded cheese mixture in with eggs.
- Turn oven down to 325 and place entire mixture into pastry shell.
- Take remaining whole steamed asparagus stalks and place on top of unbaked quiche

having the top part of the asparagus pointing towards pie shell rim ().
- Take nutmeg and sprinkle it on top of quiche evenly as possible.
- Place unbaked quiche on the center of cookie sheet and place in oven on the middle rack.
- Bake quiche at 325 degrees for 35 to 40 minutes. It's ready when a knife inserted comes out clean.
- Let quiche set for at least 10 minutes prior to serving.
- Call troops to table - serve warm or at room temperature and enjoy telling your troops how you stole the fresh eggs from the local farmer.

9. Asparagas Quiche Recipe

Serving: 6 | Prep: | Cook: 50mins | Ready in:

Ingredients

- 1/2 to 3/4 pound asparagus, trimmed, chopped
- water
- 2 tablespoons butter
- 1/2 cup chopped mushrooms
- 4 green onions, with green, thinly sliced
- 1 small tomato, peeled, seeded, diced
- 1 1/2 cups shredded havarti cheese or Swiss, about 6 ounces
- 4 large eggs
- 1 1/2 cups half-and-half or whole milk
- 1/2 teaspoon salt
- 1/8 teaspoon ground black pepper
- dash nutmeg

Direction

- In a saucepan, cover asparagus with water. Bring to a boil over high heat; reduce heat, cover, and cook for 5 minutes. Drain and set aside.
- In a skillet, heat butter over medium-low heat; add mushrooms.

- Sauté until mushrooms are tender; add green onions and cook for 1 minute longer. Set aside.
- Line a 9-inch or 10-inch pie plate with pastry; bake at 375° for 8 minutes. Remove from oven and reduce oven temperature to 350°.
- Arrange vegetables and shredded cheese in pie pastry.
- Whisk together the eggs and half-and-half; add salt, pepper, and nutmeg. Pour egg mixture over the vegetables.
- Place the filled pie shell on a large cookie sheet or jelly-roll pan.
- Place in the oven and cook for 45 to 55 minutes, or until a knife inserted in the center comes out clean.
- Serves 6 to 8.

10. Asparagus Quiche Recipe

Serving: 8 | Prep: | Cook: 37mins | Ready in:

Ingredients

- 8 ounces asparagus, washed, trimmed of all hard, tough stalks, and cut into 1 1/2 inch lengths
- 4 large eggs
- 1/4 cup whipping cream
- 1 teaspoon Dijon mustard
- 1/2 teaspoon salt
- 1/8 teaspoon cayenne pepper (or more, if desired)
- 1/4 teaspoon paprika
- 1 cup small-curd cottage cheese
- 1 cup grated Gruyére cheese
- 1/4 cup grated imported parmesan cheese

Direction

- Preheat the oven to 350 degrees. Butter a 9-inch pie plate.
- Using a small sauté pan that has a cover, heat about half a cup of water just to boiling. Pour in the sliced asparagus, cover, and turn off the heat. Allow the asparagus to steam, with the

heat turned off, while you prepare the other ingredients.
- In the large bowl of an electric mixer, beat the eggs on medium speed until they are very well blended. Blend in the cream, mustard, salt, pepper, and paprika until well combined. Using a heavy wooden spoon, stir in the cheese, stirring until they are well combined.
- Drain the asparagus (it should still be bright green, with a tender, slightly crunchy texture). Put it into the bottom of the prepared dish. Pour the egg mixture over the asparagus. And place the quiche into the oven.
- Bake for about 35 to 40 minutes, or until the quiche has puffed and browned, and is set in the center. Allow to cool 5 minutes before slicing.

11. Asparagus And Bacon Quiche Recipe

Serving: 6 | Prep: | Cook: 30mins | Ready in:

Ingredients

- 1 1/2 Pounds asparagus spears
- 8 Ounces Plain flour
- 4 Ounces butter
- 4 Tablespoons water, ice Cold
- 4 Ounces bacon, rindless, streaky, thinly sliced
- 4 Large egg yolks
- 3/4 Pint single cream
- 4 Ounces gruyere cheese, Grated
- salt and Freshly Ground white pepper, To Taste

Direction

- Pre-heat the oven to 200c/400f/gas 6.
- Trim the tips off the asparagus to the length of 1 ½ inches.
- Blanch in salted boiling water for 3 to 5 minutes then drain and refresh.
- Sift the flour into a mixing bowl along with a pinch of salt, add the butter and rub in.

- Add enough ice cold water to bind to a firm dough, turn out onto a floured surface and roll out to fit a 10 inch fluted flan dish.
- Bake blind in the oven at 190c/375f/gas 5 until set but not browned about 10-15 minutes.
- With a knife, stretch the bacon rashers on a flat surface, wrap a small piece around each asparagus tip.
- In a bowl mix the egg yolks with the cream, grated cheese and seasoning.
- Spoon onto the flan case and arrange the bacon and asparagus rolls in the custard.
- Turn the oven to 180c/350f/gas 4 and bake for 30-35 minutes or until the quiche is set and golden brown. Cool for 1 hour then serve.

12. Asparagus Pecan Quiche Recipe

Serving: 68 | Prep: | Cook: 37mins | Ready in:

Ingredients

- asparagus-Pecan Quiche
- From the cookbook Country chicken
- 1 unbaked pastry shell(9 inches) I use a homemade crust recipe I have with whole wheat flour
- 1 cup cut fresh or frozen asparagus(2 inch pieces) I used fresh
- 1 1/4 cups (5 ounces) shredded swiss cheese. I used whole slices and just tore them up.
- 1 cup cooked chicken
- 1/2 cup chopped pecans, divided
- 1/4 cup onion
- 1 tbsp flour
- 1 1/2 cups half and half cream
- 3 eggs, beaten
- 1 tsp Dijon mustard(I didn't have any Dijon so I used honey mustard)
- 1/2 tsp salt
- 3 drops hot pepper sauce(I skipped this)
- 2 tbsp grated parmesan cheese

Direction

- Line unpricked pastry shell with a double thickness of heavy duty aluminum foil. Bake at 450* for about 8 minutes or until edges just begin to Brown.
- Remove from oven and discard foil.
- Set crust aside.
- Place asparagus in a small saucepan with enough water to cover; cook until crisp-tender.
- Drain thoroughly; toss with Swiss cheese, chicken, 1/4 cup pecans, onions and flour.
- Spoon into baked crust.
- Combine cream, eggs, mustard, salt and hot pepper; pour over asparagus mixture.
- Sprinkle with Parmesan cheese. Top with remaining pecans.
- Bake at 350* for 35-40 minutes or until knife inserted near center comes out clean. Let stand 5 minutes before cutting.
- Yield: 6-8 servings

13. Awesome Tofu And Egg Quiche Recipe

Serving: 4 | Prep: | Cook: 50mins | Ready in:

Ingredients

- 1 partially baked pie shell (store bought but baked for about 10 mins)
- 1 block of tofu, crumbled
- 1/2 cup water
- dash nutmeg
- dash salt and pepper
- dash garlic powder
- 1/4 tsp hot sauce
- 4 eggs (from cage-free hens, of course!)
- 3 ounces of your favorite cheese (grated or chopped)-or however much you'd like!
- small onion, and/or 1/2 cup green pepper, and/or crumbled veggie sausage or veggie ham (I actually used onion, pepper and veg sausage in mine! It was AWESOME!)
- 1 tbs butter

- 1 tbs oil
- 2 tbs flour

Direction

- Combine tofu, eggs, water, spices and cheese in a big bowl and mix well.
- Meanwhile, in a skillet, heat your oil and butter. Sauté the onion/green pepper/or your other choices until tender.
- Pour into the bowl with the egg/tofu mixture and mix well.
- Pour into your pie shell.
- Bake at 350° for about 45 minutes. Test with a knife to make sure it's done inside the center.
- WOW!! YUMMY!

14. Bachelors Quiche Recipe

Serving: 6 | Prep: | Cook: 30mins | Ready in:

Ingredients

- 1 frozen pie crust
- 6 strips cooked bacon, broken into bits (Don't use imitation junk)
- 1 cup grated swiss cheese
- 1 cup light cream
- 3 whole eggs, minus shells. egg substitute O.K.
- dash of sea salt
- 1/2 teaspoon nutmeg
- dash of cayenne pepper

Direction

- Heat oven to 350 degrees. Toaster oven OK - just make sure heating is on "Bake".
- Thaw pie crust.
- Sprinkle bacon bits over pie crust - press some into crust.
- Spread grated cheese on top of the bacon.
- Beat eggs well (use either electric gizmo or handheld Whisk).
- Then add Cream, seasoning, Nutmeg & Cayenne pepper to eggs.

- Mix well.
- Pour into pie crust.
- Place in oven, bake for 30 minutes.
- It should be Golden Brown when done.
- Remove from oven & let cool on a Cooling Rack for approx. 10 minutes.
- Cut into wedges like a pie and enjoy. TASTES BEST WHEN HOT.
- ALTERNATIVE: Mix it up by placing your favorite veggies cut into bit sized pieces into the top half of the egg mixture before baking. Just sprinkle it on.

15. Bacon And Herb Quiche Recipe

Serving: 8 | Prep: | Cook: 35mins | Ready in:

Ingredients

- 1 3/4 cups graham flour (I use all-purpose flour)
- 1/2 cup cold butter, cubed
- 1/4 teaspoon salt
- 1/4 cup water
- 1 1/4 cups bacon, chopped and cooked
- 1 1/4 cups Emmental cheese, shredded OR cheese of your choice
- 4 large eggs
- 1/4 teaspoon salt
- 1/4 teaspoon fresh pepper
- 2 to 3 teaspoons parsley, thyme and basil, chopped
- 1 cup heavy cream

Direction

- Have prepared pie shell ready in a 9" quiche pan.
- Preheat oven to 400 degrees F.
- Combine the cooked bacon and shredded cheese in a mixing bowl.
- Whisk the eggs together in a small bowl.
- Add eggs to bacon/cheese mixture and stir.
- Add salt, pepper and herbs.
- Stir.

- Add cream.
- Using a whisk, combine all ingredients GENTLY.
- Pour egg mixture into prepared pastry shell.
- Bake for 35 minutes OR until golden on top.

16. Bacon And Leek Quiche Recipe

Serving: 6 | Prep: | Cook: 30mins | Ready in:

Ingredients

- 1 Recipe of Short Crust Pastry (Pâte Brisée)
- ½ pound bacon, cut into 1 cm (about ½-inch) cubes
- 2 leeks, white and light green parts, chopped (about 2 cups)
- 3 shallots thinly sliced
- ¼-teaspoon salt
- 1/8-teaspoon freshly ground black pepper
- 1 tablespoon Dijon mustard
- 3 eggs
- 1 cup milk
- ½ cup single cream
- ¼ pound gruyere cheese, grated (about 1 1/3-cups)
- 1 Pinch of nutmeg

Direction

- Cook the bacon in a frying pan / skillet over a low heat until just cooked, not crisp. Add the shallots, leeks, salt and freshly ground black pepper, and sauté until the leeks and shallots are soft and the bacon is crisp, about 7 to 10 minutes.
- Drain off the surplus fat, if any. Set aside.
- Preheat the oven to 375 degrees F and arrange the oven rack in the middle of the oven. Then on a liberally floured surface, roll the pastry from the centre out, lifting pastry, turning it slightly, and intermittently turning over to prevent it from sticking. Roll the pastry to 1/8-inch thickness. Lightly butter and flour a 9-inch pie dish and line with the pastry, leaving about ¼-inch overhang for shrinkage. Pinch up the surplus pastry to form an edge and flute, prick the bottom all over with a fork.
- Line the pastry case with a sheet of parchment or aluminum foil larger than the dish, and fill with pie beans (the ceramic ones are ideal for this). Bake for about 20 minutes, or until the edges begin to colour. Remove the paper and beans, and spread the mustard over the bottom of the pastry.
- Lower the oven temperature to 325 degrees F.
- In a bowl, beat the eggs lightly with the milk and cream, add a pinch of freshly ground nutmeg and then mix in the bacon and cheese mixture, pour the custard into the pie shell to within ¼-inch off the top of the crust.
- Bake 25 to 30 minutes, or until the custard is just cooked.
- Allow to cool 10 minutes before serving.
- Serving Suggestions
- My favourite is, to serve the quiche with steamed new baby potatoes tossed in butter, freshly chopped mint and parsley and with baby lettuce leaves, cucumber, spring onions finely chopped, sweet cherry tomatoes together with a little chopped red pepper. On the other hand, you could try jacket potatoes with melted butter.
- Leek is a vegetable related to the onion and garlic. Its edible portions are the white onion base and the green stalks. The white onion-like layers form around a core. I prefer to use young leeks. Otherwise discard the outer leaves; you can use them for soups.

17. Bacon Border Quiche Recipe

Serving: 6 | Prep: | Cook: 40mins | Ready in:

Ingredients

- butter
- 6 large eggs
- 1 cup heavy cream

- Several drops of hot pepper sauce, or to taste, I use Frank's red hot sauce
- salt and pepper to taste (I leave out the salt)
- 3 oz. can of diced green chillies, I used 4 oz. can
- 1/4 pound chorizo, crumbled, fried and drained, I used 8 slices of Hearty Thick Cut bacon instead.
- 1 cup diced muenster cheese
- 1/3 cup chopped fresh cilantro (I skipped)
- 1/3 cup chopped scallions (I used a bit of regular onion)

Direction

- Preheat the oven to 350 degrees.
- Have ready a buttered 8-inch quiche pan.
- Beat the eggs in a bowl with the cream, hot pepper sauce, and salt and pepper.
- Add the remaining ingredients, mix well, and pour into the quiche pan.
- Bake 40 minutes, or until golden brown on top.
- Serve hot, warm, or at room temperature.

18. Bacon Green Chili Quiche Recipe

Serving: 6 | Prep: | Cook: 40mins | Ready in:

Ingredients

- 1 pound bacon
- 1 carton chopped green chilies
- 1 cup grated jack cheese
- 1-1/2 cups milk
- 1 cup baking mix
- 6 ounces sour cream
- 3 eggs
- 1 teaspoon salt
- 2 teaspoons freshly ground black pepper

Direction

- Brown drain and crumble bacon then put in bottom of greased pie plate.
- Top with onion and cheese.
- Put remaining ingredients in blender for 1 minute then pour over onion and cheese.
- Bake at 350 for 40 minutes.

19. Bacon Ham And Swiss Cheese Quiche Recipe

Serving: 6 | Prep: | Cook: 30mins | Ready in:

Ingredients

- 6 strips of lean bacon
- 1 cup chopped peeled onion
- 1 (9-inch) unbaked pie crust
- 1/2 cup shredded swiss cheese
- 1 1/2 cups whipping cream
- 4 large eggs
- 1/2 teaspoon salt
- 1/4 teaspoon ground nutmeg
- 1/8 teaspoon ground white pepper
- 1/2 cup diced cooked ham

Direction

- Preheat oven to 350°F.
- Cook bacon in a medium skillet until crisp.
- Remove from pan and drain on paper towels; crumble.
- Drain all but 1 tablespoon of fat from skillet.
- Sauté onion over medium-high heat until tender, about 4 minutes; set aside.
- Sprinkle crumbled bacon on the bottom of unbaked pie crust.
- Top with onion and cheese.
- In a medium bowl, whisk together cream, eggs, salt, nutmeg and pepper until well blended.
- Stir in ham.
- Pour into pie crust and bake for 30 minutes, or until center is set.
- Hint:

- Adding some chopped young spinach leaves to this quiche makes it an extra-tasty, and extra-HEALTHY meal!

20. Bacon Lobster Quiche Recipe

Serving: 4 | Prep: | Cook: 30mins | Ready in:

Ingredients

- 9 inch pie crust unbaked
- 4 slices bacon
- 2 cups lobster meat
- 1/4 cup scallions sliced
- 1 cup swiss cheese shredded
- 3 eggs
- 1/2 cup milk
- 1/2 cup heavy cream
- 1/2 teaspoon salt
- 1/8 teaspoon freshly ground black pepper
- 1/8 teaspoon nutmeg

Direction

- Preheat oven to 375 then line a quiche or pine pan with pie crust.
- Cook bacon until crisp and set on paper towel to drain.
- Layer half of the lobster meat, scallions and Swiss cheese in pie crust.
- Repeat process for remaining half.
- Beat eggs then add milk, cream, salt, pepper and nutmeg and pour over lobster mixture.
- Crumble bacon into small pieces and sprinkle on top then bake 30 minutes.

21. Bacon Onion Quiche Recipe

Serving: 8 | Prep: | Cook: 45mins | Ready in:

Ingredients

- 1 cup all purpose flour
- 1/4 teaspoon salt
- 1/4 cup butter softened
- 1 egg
- Filling:
- 1 tablespoon peanut oil
- 5 ounces smoked bacon thinly sliced
- 2 tablespoons butter
- 1 medium white onion sliced
- 2 ounces gruyere cheese grated
- 3/4 cup light cream
- 2 eggs
- 1/8 teaspoon salt
- 1/4 teaspoon freshly ground black pepper
- 1/3 teaspoon grated nutmeg

Direction

- Mound flour on a work surface then sprinkle salt over it and make well in center.
- Cut butter into small pieces and put in well with 1 egg.
- Mix with fingers from center outwards working quickly and not kneading too much.
- As soon as it no longer sticks to your fingers roll it into a ball and put in a plastic bag.
- Refrigerate 15 minutes then roll out dough on a work surface.
- Butter a tart pan and line with dough.
- Prick several times with a fork without piercing dough right through.
- Refrigerate 25 minutes or until firm.
- To make filling heat oil in a non-stick skillet and brown bacon strips quickly.
- Remove and set aside on a plate then wipe out pan and melt butter in it.
- Add onion and quickly brown then set aside on a second plate.
- Preheat oven to 450.
- Take pastry shell from refrigerator and cover with the onions.
- Scatter bacon strips over the top and sprinkle with grated cheese.
- Pour cream into a saucepan and bring just to a simmer.
- Break remaining eggs into a ceramic or glass bowl and beat with a fork.

- Gradually beat in hot cream, salt, pepper and nutmeg.
- Carefully pour this mixture into the tart shell.
- Bake 45 minutes then remove from oven and let rest 10 minutes before serving.

22. Bacon Quiche Biscuit Cups Recipe

Serving: 10 | Prep: | Cook: 21mins | Ready in:

Ingredients

- 5 slices bacon, crisply cooked and finely crumbled
- 1 package (8 oz) cream cheese, softened
- 2 tablespoons milk
- 2 eggs
- 1/2 cup shredded swiss cheese (2 oz)
- 2 tablespoons chopped green onions (2 medium)
- 1 can (12 oz) Pillsbury® Golden Lays® refrigerated biscuits (10 biscuits)

Direction

- Heat oven to 375F. Grease 10 muffin cups. In a small bowl, beat cream cheese, milk and eggs on low speed until smooth. Stir in Swiss cheese and green onions; set aside.
- Separate dough into 10 biscuits. Place 1 biscuit in each greased muffin cup; firmly press in bottom and up sides, forming 1/4 inch rim. Place bacon in the bottom of the dough -lined muffin cups. Spoon about 2 tablespoons of the cheese mixture over the bacon.
- Bake for 21 to 26 minutes or until filling is set and edges of biscuits are golden brown.

23. Bacon Spinach Quiche Recipe

Serving: 8 | Prep: | Cook: 50mins | Ready in:

Ingredients

- 6 slices bacon cooked and crumbled with fat retained in pan
- 1/4 cup white onion minced finely
- 1 teaspoon basil
- 3/4 pound shredded swiss cheese
- 10 ounce package spinach thawed and squeezed dry
- 1/4 cup fresh mushrooms sliced
- 1-1/2 cups heavy cream
- 5 eggs well beaten
- 2 tablespoons brown mustard

Direction

- Add basil and onions to bacon fat and sauté 10 minutes until tender.
- Whisk eggs, mustard and cream.
- In buttered quiche dish layer cheese, spinach, mushrooms, onion mixture and bacon.
- Pour egg mixture over everything being careful to cover all the layers.
- Bake at 325 for 50 minutes then cool slightly and serve while warm.

24. Bacon And Corn Quiche Recipe

Serving: 6 | Prep: | Cook: 40mins | Ready in:

Ingredients

- 1 unbaked pie shell for 10-inch pie plate
- ¦6 slices bacon, cooked and crumbled, or 1/2 cup diced ham
- ¦1 cup grated Swiss or monterey jack cheese
- ¦1/2 cup minced scallions
- ¦1/4 cup diced red or yellow pepper (optional)
- ¦4 eggs
- ¦1 cup corn kernels
- ¦1 cup light cream
- ¦salt and pepper, to taste
- ¦dash of nutmeg

Direction

- Preheat oven to 425 degrees F. Line a 10-inch pie plate or quiche form with pastry, and partially bake for about 8 minutes.
- Sprinkle the crumbled bacon, cheese, scallions, and pepper into the pie pan. Beat the eggs slightly, then beat the remaining ingredients into the eggs and pour the mixture into the pie plate.
- Bake for 10 minutes. Reduce the heat to 300 degrees F and bake for 30 to 40 minutes, or until a knife tests clean.
- Let rest for 10 minutes before cutting.

25. Bacon And Leek Quiche Recipe

Serving: 6 | Prep: | Cook: 30mins | Ready in:

Ingredients

- One Recipe of Short Crust Pastry (Pâte Brisée)
- ½ pound bacon, cut into 1 cm (about ½-inch) cubes
- 2 leeks, white and light green parts, chopped (about 2 cups)
- 3 shallots thinly sliced
- ¼-teaspoon salt
- 1/8-teaspoon freshly ground black pepper
- 1-tablespoon Dijon mustard
- 3 eggs
- 1-cup milk
- ½-cup single cream
- ¼ pound gruyere cheese, grated (about 1 1/3-cups)
- 1 Pinch of nutmeg

Direction

- Cook the bacon in a frying pan / skillet over a low heat until just cooked, not crisp. Add the shallots, leeks, salt and freshly ground black pepper and sauté until the leeks and shallots are soft and the bacon is crisp, about 7 to 10 minutes.
- Drain off the surplus fat, if any. Set aside.
- Preheat the oven to 375 degrees F and arrange the oven rack in the middle of the oven. Then on a liberally floured surface, roll the pastry from the centre out, lifting pastry, turning it slightly, and intermittently turning over to prevent it from sticking. Roll the pastry to 1/8-inch thickness. Lightly butter and flour a 9-inch pie dish and line with the pastry, leaving about ¼-inch overhang for shrinkage. Pinch up the surplus pastry to form an edge and flute, prick the bottom all over with a fork.
- Line the pastry case with a sheet of parchment or aluminium foil larger than the dish, and fill with pie beans (the ceramic ones are ideal for this). Bake for about 20 minutes, or until the edges begin to colour. Remove the paper and beans, and spread the mustard over the bottom of the pastry.
- Lower the oven temperature to 325 degrees F.
- In a bowl, beat the eggs lightly with the milk and cream, add a pinch of freshly ground nutmeg and then mix in the bacon and cheese mixture, pour the custard into the pie shell to within ¼-inch off the top of the crust.
- Bake 25 to 30 minutes, or until the custard is just cooked.
- Allow to cool 10 minutes before serving.
- Serve warm or room temperature.
- Serving Suggestions
- My favourite is, to serve the quiche with steamed new baby potatoes tossed in butter, freshly chopped mint, and parsley and with baby lettuce leaves, cucumber, spring onions finely chopped, sweet cherry tomatoes together with a little chopped red pepper. On the other hand, you could try jacket potatoes with melted butter.
- Leek is a vegetable related to the onion and garlic. Its edible portions are the white onion base and the green stalks. The white onion-like layers form around a core. I prefer to use young leeks. Otherwise discard the outer leaves; you can use them for soups.

26. Bacon And Mushroom Bite Size Quiche Recipe

Serving: 42 | Prep: | Cook: 20mins | Ready in:

Ingredients

- 8 slices bacon
- 1/4 pound fresh mushrooms, chopped
- 1 tablespoon butter
- 1/3 cup chopped green onion
- 1 2/3 cups shredded swiss cheese
- 1 15-oz. package prepared pie crusts (2 crusts)
- 5 eggs
- 1 2/3 cups sour cream

Direction

- Heat oven to 375 degrees F. On a lightly floured board, roll out the pastry dough 1/ 16-inch thick. Using a 3-inch cutter, cut out 42 circles; re-roll scraps as needed. Fit circles into bottoms and slightly up sides of lightly greased 2 1/2-inch muffin pans. Meanwhile, fry bacon slices until crisp, drain; crumble or chop. Chop mushrooms, sauté in butter until limp and liquid evaporates. Combine bacon, mushrooms, green onion and cheese. Divide filling equally among muffin cups. In large bowl, beat together eggs, add sour cream and stir until smooth. Spoon about 1 tablespoon into each muffin cup. Bake until puffed and light brown, 20-25 minutes. Cool in pans 5 minutes; lift out. Serve warm or let cool on wire racks. If made ahead, wrap cooled quiches airtight, and refrigerate overnight. Reheat, uncovered, in a 350 degrees F. oven for about 10 minutes.
- Makes 3 1/2 dozen.

27. Bacon And Swiss Quiche Recipe

Serving: 6 | Prep: | Cook: 50mins | Ready in:

Ingredients

- 2 pieces phyllo dough cut into 3 strips each
- 3 large eggs
- 1/4 cup egg substitute
- 1 cup evaporated milk
- 2 tablespoons all purpose flour
- 1/4 teaspoon salt
- 1/4 teaspoon freshly ground black pepper
- 1/4 teaspoon ground nutmeg
- 1/2 cup swiss cheese grated
- 4 ounces cooked crisp bacon diced

Direction

- Preheat oven to 350 then coat pie plate with cooking spray.
- Gently lay dough in pie plate one piece at a time coating each layer with cooking spray.
- Whisk eggs, egg substitute, milk, flour, salt, pepper and nutmeg.
- Sprinkle cheese and bacon over dough then pour in egg mixture.
- Place on baking sheet and bake until firm then allow to cool and cut into wedges.

28. Bacon, (butternut) Squash And Feta Cheese Tart Recipe

Serving: 6 | Prep: | Cook: 40mins | Ready in:

Ingredients

- CRUST:
- 500 g short crust pastry
- FILLING:
- 15ml oil
- packet of diced bacon
- 250 ml double thick cream/ normal cream also works fine
- small bunch of parsley chopped up
- salt
- pepper
- 100 g feta cheese
- 2 eggs
- 2 cloves of finely chopped garlic

- 300 g butternut squash cubed and cooked
- grated cheese

Direction

- Pre heat oven to 170 C
- Grease a pie tin or oven proof pie dish. Roll out pastry until it's large enough to line the tin/dish with and that the pastry edges sits slightly above the rim. Prick the pastry base with a fork.
- Bake pastry for about 10- 15 minutes and take out of oven.
- While pastry is baking, fry bacon until golden.
- Beat together cream and eggs with garlic and parsley with salt and pepper for seasoning.
- Arrange butternut squash pieces with the bacon and feta n pastry pie dish and pour the cream-egg mixture over it. And sprinkle some grated cheese over the mixture.
- Bake for about 20 -25 minutes until golden and softly set.
- Enjoy warm or cold!
- (A great variation to this tart is to add spinach)

29. Bankheads Quiche Lorraine Recipe

Serving: 6 | Prep: | Cook: 50mins | Ready in:

Ingredients

- 9" frozen deep dish pie shell
- 2.8 oz package real bacon bits (or 10 slices bacon cooked & crumbled)
- 1/4 cup chopped onion
- 8 oz shredded swiss cheese, divided
- 6 beaten eggs
- 1 cup fat free half & half
- 1/2 tsp salt
- dash red pepper
- dash white pepepr
- 1/8 tsp ground nutmeg

Direction

- Thaw pie shell for 15 minutes.
- Prick bottom and sides of shell with fork a few times.
- Bake directly on oven rack for 10 min. at temp. on the package.
- Sauté onion (and bacon if using real) until browned and drain well.
- Sprinkle evenly in shell.
- Top with 1 cup cheese and set aside.
- Combine eggs, milk and spices, stirring well.
- Pour into shell and top with remaining cheese.
- Bake on cookie sheet at 350 degrees for 50 minutes until set.
- Let stand 10 minutes before serving.

30. Basil Tomato And Mozarella Mini Quiches Recipe

Serving: 8 | Prep: | Cook: 40mins | Ready in:

Ingredients

- Dough
- 2 cups all pusposeflour
- 1 teaspoon salt
- ¾ cup shortenng or butter
- 5 to 6tablespoons cold water
- Filling
- 3 large eggs
- 1cup cream
- 1cup milk
- salt , pepper and nutmeg
- 1 tomato cuted in little squares
- ½ cup fresh basil leaves
- 1/3 cup Mozarella cuted into cubes
- ¼ cup grated parmesan cheese

Direction

- Dough for Pie Crust
- Preheat oven at 375 F.
- In food processor with knife blade attached, measure flour, shortening and salt. Process 1 to 2 seconds until mixture form fine crumbs.

Add cold water, process 1, to 2 seconds until dough forms on blades. Remove dough rom bowl; with hands, shape dough into ball.

- Line each pie pan and bake for about 15 - 20 minutes.
- Filling
- In a small bowl cook the tomato and basil for about 5 minutes in a medium low heat.
- Fill each mini pie crust and add mozzarella cheese.
- In the blender mix eggs, cream, milk, salt, pepper and nutmeg.
- Pour over each mini quiche and spread grated Parmesan cheese over each one.
- Bake for about 25 – 30 minutes and ready!
- Serve warm.

31. Bears Seafood Quiche Recipe

Serving: 12 | Prep: | Cook: 65mins | Ready in:

Ingredients

- ½ teaspoon seasoned salt
- 2 tablespoons flour
- ½ cup mayonnaise
- 4 eggs - extra large or jumbo
- 2 cups milk (2% ok)
- 1 cup Mozzarella & swiss cheese - shredded
- 1 cup cheddar cheese - shredded
- 1 tin crab meat
- 1 tin tiny shrimp
- ½ cup chopped green onions
- ½ teaspoon dry mustard
- 3 or 4 drops red hot sauce
- 3 regular or 2 deep dish pie shells

Direction

- Mix ingredients together in mixer, beating eggs and milk first.
- Pour into pie shells.
- Bake on a cookie sheet at 350° for one hour.
- Let stand 5 minutes.
- Each pie serves 6 people.

32. Biltong And Cheese Quiche Beef Jerky Recipe

Serving: 8 | Prep: | Cook: 45mins | Ready in:

Ingredients

- 150g cake flour - 5.2 oz
- big pinch salt
- 1 tsp mustard powder
- 120g butter - 4.2 oz
- 50ml iced water - 1.7 fl oz
- FILLING
- 2 leeks sliced
- 1 tbl spoon butter
- 1 tbls oil
- 2 tbls chopped fennel or parsley
- 120g grated biltong - beef jerky 4.2oz
- 4 beaten eggs
- 250ml cream - 8.8 fl oz
- 150ml sour cream - 5.2 fl oz
- 100g grated cheese - 3.5 oz
- 1 tsp mustard powder
- 1 tbls lemon juice
- 1 tsp lemon rind, grated
- freshly ground black pepper

Direction

- Sift flour and salt together.
- Cut in butter till it resembles fine breadcrumbs.
- Add iced water to form a soft dough.
- Place in a plastic bag and let rest in fridge for at least half an hour.
- Roll out on a floured board and then line a 230 mm quiche dish.
- Bake blind in a 200C, 400F gas 6 oven for 8-10 min.
- Gently fry leaks in butter and oil till soft.
- Spread over bottom of pastry shell.
- Mix rest of ingredients and pour into pastry shell.

- Bake for 35-45 min in a 160C, 300F gas 2 oven.

33. Blue Cheese Crab Quiche Recipe

Serving: 8 | Prep: | Cook: 45mins | Ready in:

Ingredients

- 1 prepared pie crust
- 1 cup imitation crab crumbled
- 1/4 cup blue cheese crumbled
- 1 cup shredded mozzarella cheese
- 1 green onion chopped fine
- 1/8 teaspoon freshly ground black pepper
- 4 eggs
- 1 cup milk
- 1/2 cup parmesan

Direction

- Preheat oven to 350.
- Spread crab, cheeses and onions in crust.
- Whisk together eggs, milk and pepper and pour slowly into crust.
- Sprinkle with parmesan and bake for 35 minutes
- Allow to set 5 minutes before serving.

34. Broccoli Ham And Cheese Quiche Recipe

Serving: 68 | Prep: | Cook: 5mins | Ready in:

Ingredients

- broccoli ham and cheese Quiche
- ½ cup shredded cheddar cheese
- ¼ cup shredded monterey jack cheese
- ¼ cup mozzarella cheese
- 1 can (10 ¾ oz.) regular OR fat free condensed broccoli cheese soup

- 5 eggs
- ¼ tsp.garlic powder or 2 gloves, minced
- 1 package (10 oz.) frozen chopped broccoli
- 1 small onion, finely chopped
- 1 cup diced cooked ham
- 1 9- inch baked deep dish pie crust

Direction

- Pre heat oven to 350.
- Mix Cheddar cheese, Monterey Jack cheese and mozzarella cheese. Set aside.
- In a medium bowl mix soup, eggs, garlic powder, broccoli, onion, ham, and ½ cup cheese mixture. Pour into cooked pie crust.
- Bake at 350 for 45 minutes or until knife inserted in center comes out clean, Sprinkle with remaining cheese and bake 5 minutes more. Let stand 5 minutes before cutting.

35. Broccoli Quiche Recipe

Serving: 8 | Prep: | Cook: 45mins | Ready in:

Ingredients

- 1 1/2 cups frozen broccoli, steamed until tender
- 1/2 cup sliced mushrooms (I used portabello, white would be fine)
- 1 med. onion, chopped
- 3-4 cloves garlic, minced
- 3 eggs
- 1 egg yolk
- 1 cup heavy cream
- 1 cup shredded cheddar, divided
- 3 pieces cooked bacon, crumbled
- salt and pepper
- 2 tbs. olive oil
- 2 tbs. butter
- 1 frozen pie crust, or your own homemade

Direction

- Preheat oven to 375 degrees.

- In sauté pan, melt butter, add olive oil. Add chopped onion, garlic and mushrooms, cook until just tender (3-5 minutes). Add broccoli (previously steamed and tossed with salt and pepper to taste), heat through. Remove from heat, set aside.
- Whisk together cream, eggs, egg yolk and 3/4 cup of the shredded cheese. Add about a teaspoon of salt and 8 twists of the pepper grinder to this mixture. Don't overdo it, but you don't want it bland, either.
- Layer the remaining 1/4 cup of shredded cheese onto the crust. Top with the broccoli mixture. Pour over all the cream/egg mixture and with wooden spoon, gently mix down into the vegetables. Top with crumbled bacon pieces.
- Bake for 45 minutes, or until knife inserted in center comes out clean.
- Enjoy!

36. Broccoli Rice Quiche Recipe

Serving: 3 | Prep: | Cook: 30mins | Ready in:

Ingredients

- 1 1/2 cups cooked brown rice; hot
- 3 ounces sharp Cheddar cheese; grated
- 3 whole eggs
- 3 ounces skim milk
- 3/4 cup canned mushrooms; drained
- 1 1/2 cups Broccoli; cooked and chopped
- 1/2 teaspoon salt
- 1/8 teaspoon pepper

Direction

- Combine hot rice, one beaten egg, 1/4 teaspoon salt and half of the cheese.
- Spoon into a 9" pie pan that has been sprayed with Pam, press against the sides and bottom to form a shell.

- Beat the remaining 2 eggs, stir in milk, mushrooms, broccoli, remaining salt and pepper.
- Spoon into rice shell.
- Bake at 375 degrees for 20 minutes, then sprinkle remaining cheese on top and bake for 10 more minutes.
- Let stand for 5 minutes before cutting.
- Makes 3 servings.

37. Broccoli And Cheddar Mini Quiches Recipe

Serving: 4 | Prep: | Cook: 25mins | Ready in:

Ingredients

- 2 cups broccoli florets
- 1c milk(do not use skim)
- 2 lg. eggs plus 2 lg egg yolks
- 1c heavy cream
- 1c grated cheddar cheese
- 1/2tsp. salt
- 1/2tsp. pepper
- 1/4tsp. ground nutmeg

Direction

- Preheat oven to 350 and line a large rimmed baking sheet with foil. Grease 8 cups in a 12c muffin tin and set aside. Pour 1" of water into a large saucepan and put in steamer basket. Place broccoli in basket, cover pot, turn heat to high and let cook until broccoli is just tender, 5-6 minutes. Let broccoli cool slightly then chop into small pieces.
- In a medium bowl, whisk together milk, cream, eggs and egg yolks. Stir in cheese, salt, pepper and nutmeg. Add chopped broccoli.
- Put muffin tin on baking sheet, then ladle egg mixture into prepared muffin cups, filling each cup. Bake until lightly brown and no longer jiggly in center, about 25 mins. Let cool slightly then run a knife around each quiche.

Put a clean baking sheet on top of muffin pan and invert to unmold quiches.

- Serve warm or at room temperature.

38. Broccoli And Blue Cheese Quiche Recipe

Serving: 6 | Prep: | Cook: 30mins | Ready in:

Ingredients

- Pastry:
- 2 boiled and peeled potatoes, cold
- 50 g butter
- 100 ml plain flour
- 100 ml whole wheat flour
- Filling:
- 300 g broccoli florets
- 1 small leek, sliced
- ½ tsp butter
- 50 g light blue cheese
- 2 eggs
- 1 tsp Dijon mustard
- 200 ml milk
- ½ tsp fine sea salt
- ¼ tsp freshly ground pepper
- grated cheese

Direction

- Heat oven to 200°C.
- Grate potatoes and mix with butter and flours in food processor. Wrap in cling film and let the dough rest in the fridge for 10-15 min before lining a flan dish and blind baking for 10 min.
- Meanwhile, steam broccoli, sauté leek in butter and mix eggs, mustard, milk and season.
- Add broccoli and leeks to the flan crust and crumble over the blue cheese. Pour over the egg mixture and scatter some grated cheese on top.
- Bake in oven 20-25 min until the egg mixture is cooked.

39. CHEESE AND CHILE QUICHE Recipe

Serving: 6 | Prep: | Cook: 90mins | Ready in:

Ingredients

- pastry dough
- 1 large garlic clove
- 3/4 teaspoon salt
- 1 lb poblano chiles (about 4 large), roasted and peeled
- 6 large eggs
- 1 cup whole milk
- 1/2 cup Mexican crema or heavy cream
- 2 tablespoons finely grated white onion (using small teardrop holes of a box grater)
- 1/2 teaspoon black pepper
- 1/2 lb monterey jack cheese, coarsely grated (2 1/2 to 3 cups)

Direction

- Put oven rack in middle position and preheat oven to 375°F.
- Roll out dough into a 13-inch round on a lightly floured surface with a floured rolling pin. Fit dough into tart pan, without stretching, letting excess dough hang over edge. Fold overhang inward and press against side of pan to reinforce edge. Prick bottom all over with a fork. Chill until firm, about 30 minutes.
- Line shell with foil or parchment paper and fill with pie weights. Bake until pastry is set and pale golden along rim, 20 to 25 minutes.
- Carefully remove foil and weights and bake shell until deep golden all over, 15 to 20 minutes more. Put tart pan in a shallow baking pan. Leave oven on.
- Mince garlic and mash to a paste with salt using side of a large knife.
- Discard seeds, ribs, and stems from chilies, then pat dry if necessary and cut into 1/3-inch-wide strips.

- Whisk together eggs, milk, cream, onion, garlic paste, and pepper in a large bowl until just combined, then pour into baked tart shell.
- Sprinkle cheese and chilies over custard (chilies will sink slightly) and bake until custard is just set, 50 to 60 minutes. (Center will jiggle slightly; filling will continue to set as it cools.)
- Transfer quiche in pan to a rack to cool at least 20 minutes before serving.
- To remove side of tart pan, center a large can under pan and let side of pan drop. Serve warm or at room temperature.
- Cooks' notes:
- • Quiche can be baked 1 day ahead and chilled, covered.
- • Reheat, uncovered, in a 325°F oven until just heated through, about 25 minutes.

40. CHEESEBURGER QUICHE Recipe

Serving: 6 | Prep: | Cook: 38mins | Ready in:

Ingredients

- 1 pound lean ground beef
- 1 small onion, diced
- 6 pieces crisp bacon, crumbled (or more!)
- 3 eggs
- 1/2 cup mayonnaise
- 1/2 cup heavy cream
- garlic powder
- salt, to taste
- pepper, to taste
- 8 ounces sharp cheddar, shredded

Direction

- Preheat oven to 350 degrees F.
- Brown ground beef and onion together in a skillet.
- Break meat up into small "crumbs" (I use a pastry cutter)
- Drain fat from skillet.

- Add bacon.
- Press meat mixture into a deep dish pie pan.
- VOILA, quiche crust!
- Whisk together the eggs, mayonnaise, cream, garlic powder and salt and pepper, to taste.
- Fold the shredded cheddar into the egg mixture.
- Pour mixture over the "crust".
- Bake for 35 to 40 minutes.

41. Cajun Quiche Recipe

Serving: 4 | Prep: | Cook: 30mins | Ready in:

Ingredients

- Crust:
- 2 cups cooked long-grain white rice, cooled
- 1 teaspoon garlic powder
- 1 teaspoon onion powder
- 1/2 teaspoon salt
- 1 large egg
- cooking spray
- 1/4 cup (1 ounce) reduced-fat shredded cheddar cheese
- ====================================
- Filling:
- 1/2 cup prechopped onion
- 1/2 cup prechopped celery
- 1/2 cup prechopped red bell pepper
- 1 teaspoon bottled minced garlic
- 3 ounces andouille sausage or kielbasa, chopped (about 2/3 cup)
- 3/4 cup egg substitute
- 1/4 cup plain fat-free yogurt
- 1/4 teaspoon salt
- 1/4 teaspoon hot pepper sauce (such as Tabasco)
- 2 large egg whites
- 1/4 cup (1 ounce) reduced-fat shredded cheddar cheese

Direction

- Preheat oven to 375°.
- To prepare crust, combine rice, garlic powder, onion powder, 1/2 teaspoon salt, and 1 egg. Spread mixture into the bottom and up sides of a 9-inch pie plate coated with cooking spray. Sprinkle bottom of crust evenly with 1/4 cup shredded cheddar cheese.
- To prepare filling, heat a medium non-stick skillet over medium-high heat. Coat pan with cooking spray. Add onion and the next 4 ingredients (through sausage); sauté 5 minutes. Spoon mixture evenly into prepared rice crust.
- Combine the egg substitute, fat-free yogurt, salt, hot pepper sauce, and egg whites; stir with a whisk until well blended. Pour egg substitute mixture over sausage mixture. Sprinkle with 1/4 cup shredded cheddar cheese.
- Bake at 375° for 30 minutes or until the center is set. Let stand 5 minutes before serving.

42. California Quiche Recipe

Serving: 8 | Prep: | Cook: 45mins | Ready in:

Ingredients

- 1 9-inch deep dish pie shell, unbaked
- 4 eggs
- 1/2 cup sour cream
- 1 cup half & half
- 1 cup chicken, cooked & cubed
- 1 cup colby Jack cheese, grated
- 1 can diced green chilies
- 1 tablespoon flour
- salt and pepper to taste

Direction

- Preheat oven to 350 degrees.
- In a medium bowl, beat together the eggs, sour cream, half-and-half and flour. Stir in remaining ingredients.

- Pour mixture into pie crust. Bake for 45 minutes to 1 hour or until the top is golden brown.

43. Canadian Bacon Potato Quiche Recipe

Serving: 8 | Prep: | Cook: 50mins | Ready in:

Ingredients

- 1 refrigerated pie crust
- 1 C country style diced potatoes, thawed
- 1 C ½ inch pieces of fresh asparagus
- 1 C diced Canadian bacon
- 1 ½ C havarti, shredded (6 oz)
- 4 eggs
- 1 C milk
- ½ t marjoram
- ¼ t salt

Direction

- 375 oven
- Prepare crust as directed on package
- Bake about 8 minutes or until golden
- Layer potatoes, asparagus, bacon and cheese in partially baked crust
- Beat eggs, milk, marjoram & salt, blend well
- Pour over mixture in pie shell
- Bake 40 – 50 minutes or until knife comes out clean
- Let stand 5 minutes
- 8 servings

44. Caramelized Onion And Bacon Mini Quiches Recipe

Serving: 12 | Prep: | Cook: 20mins | Ready in:

Ingredients

- 1 recipe of your favorite two-crust pie crust recipe or 1 pkg. pre-made pie crust sheets (2 sheets)
- 2 tsp. oil
- 1 large onion, finely chopped
- 4 oz. bacon, finely chopped
- 2 tsp. whole-grain mustard
- couple pinches black pepper
- 2 eggs
- 1/2 c. milk

Direction

- Preheat oven to 400 degrees F. Grease two round mini-muffin pans (24 holes, total).
- Roll out dough to about 1/8 inch thick, or if using package dough, unroll sheets. Cut 24 rounds total from dough with 3-inch cutter. Line each mini-muffin tin with a dough circle. Cover with dishtowel and set aside while preparing filling.
- Heat oil in a large skillet. Add onion, cover and cook over medium-low heat for 30 minutes, or until golden (caramelized onion is slow-cooked to bring out the sweetness, so don't rush this step). Transfer to a bowl to cool.
- Add bacon to the pan and cook until crisp. Mix with the onion. Add mustard and season with pepper. Place a small amount of mixture in each pastry shell, using all of mixture.
- In a small bowl or cup with spout, whisk eggs; add mild and whisk until combined. Pour a small amount over each pastry shell over onion/bacon mixture.
- Bake for 15 - 20 minutes or until puffed and golden. Serve warm or at room temperature.

45. Caribbean Chicken Mango Quiche W Golden Jewel Cous Cous Crust Recipe

Serving: 6 | Prep: | Cook: 45mins | Ready in:

Ingredients

- 2 Cups Golden Jewel Blend
- As needed   chicken stock
- ¼ Cup panko bread crumbs
- 1 Tbsp butter, unsalted
- 1 ea 5 oz chicken breast
- 1 Tbsp olive oil
- 2 oz yellow onions, minced
- 2 cloves garlic, peeled & minced
- 6 ea large eggs
- ¾ Cup   whole milk
- ½ Cup   coconut milk
- ½ Cup   goats cheese, crumbled
- 1 ea   fresh mango, small dice
- 1 Tbsp   caribbean jerk seasoning
- 1/3 Cup picked cilantro
- To taste   salt & pepper

Direction

- Preheat BBQ grill and Preheat Oven to 350°F.
- Follow instructions on package for Golden Jewel Blend Couscous. Cook completely and let cool. Melt the butter and add it to the Golden Jewel blend along with the Panko bread crumbs. Place the Golden Jewel Blend into an 8" pie plate. Press it down and up the sides of the dish about ¼ inch thick; it is ok to crush the Golden Jewel Blend just a little.
- Par bake crust for 15 minutes in 350 degree oven until golden!
- Grill off chicken breast for a great smoky flavor. Let cool and then shred it to bite size pieces.
- While chicken is cooking to an internal temperature of 155°, sauté the onions and garlic until onions are translucent, add shredded chicken and toss in a bowl with jerk seasoning, picked cilantro and mango. Add mixture to the Golden Jewel Blend Crust in the 8" pie plate.
- In a small bowl mix eggs, milk and coconut milk well and pour over other ingredients in the Golden Jewel Blend Crust.
- Top with crumbled goat cheese and bake for 45 minutes or until eggs set, at 350°F

Uncover. Preheat oven to 350° F. Bake for 60 minutes or until warmed. Sprinkle with extra cheese before serving if desired.

46. Cauliettes Mushroom Gratin Recipe

Serving: 4 | Prep: | Cook: 35mins | Ready in:

Ingredients

- For the skinny "Alfredo" sauce:
- • 1/2 (14 oz) package Mann's cauliflower Cauliettes
- • 3/4 cup milk or vegetable broth
- • 1/4 cup grated Parmesan cheese• 1/4 tsp salt
- • 1/4 tsp garlic powder
- • Dash cayenne pepper
- For the Gratin:
- • 1/2 (14 oz) Mann's cauliflower Cauliettes
- • 1/4 cup onion, diced
- • 2 tsp olive oil, divided
- • 1 1/2 cup sliced mushrooms
- • 1/2 cup shredded mozzarella cheese

Direction

- 1. Microwave Cauliettes covered for 6 minutes, until very soft. Split the Cauliettes in half and use half for the sauce and half for the main ingredients. Sauté onion until soft, then set aside. Sauté mushrooms in olive oil until slightly brown, then set aside.
- 2. Pre-heat oven to 350°F. Purée all the sauce ingredients in food processor or blender until very smooth. Set aside.
- 3. Mix cooked Cauliettes, cooked onions, and cooked mushrooms with sauce. Spread in shallow baking dish (8" to 10" diameter).
- 4. Sprinkle cheese on top. Bake for 20 minutes, until bubbling at edges and starting to turn golden brown on top.
- For freeze ahead: Prepare as above using two 2-quart casserole dishes. Allow dish to cool to room temperature. Cover tightly with plastic wrap, then with aluminum foil; freeze for up to two months. Thaw overnight in refrigerator.

47. Chavrie Spinach Quiche Recipe

Serving: 8 | Prep: | Cook: 45mins | Ready in:

Ingredients

- 1pkg. (5.3 oz.) Chavrie goat cheese
- 4 eggs
- 6 oz. heavy cream or (Alouette crème fraiche)
- 6 oz. Half and Half
- ½ tsp cayenne
- ½ tsp. salt
- ¼ tsp. Ground white pepper
- 1 9 inch pie crust pre-baked
- 1 pkg. frozen spinach, thawed and drained
- 1 pinch nutmeg

Direction

- Blend Chavrie with eggs and mix well.
- Add cream and half and half to make custard and season with salt, pepper, cayenne and nutmeg.
- Scatter the spinach evenly over the bottom of the pre-baked piecrust.
- Pour custard into the shell stirring with a fork to evenly distribute the spinach.
- Bake at 350° F for 45 minutes, until a knife blade inserted into it comes out clean.
- Let rest and serve warm.
- Variations:
- Substitute Spinach with 12 oz. fresh diced asparagus.

48. Chicken Almond Quiche Dated 1966 Recipe

Serving: 8 | Prep: | Cook: 30mins | Ready in:

Ingredients

- 9-inch unbaked pie shell
- 1/2 cup diced chicken
- 3 tablespoons sliced almonds
- 1-1/2 cup shredded swiss cheese
- 2 eggs beaten
- 1-1/2 cups milk
- 1/2 teaspoon salt
- 1/4 teaspoon mace
- 1/8 teaspoon pepper
- 2 tablespoons grated parmesan cheese

Direction

- Put chicken, almonds, Swiss cheese in pie shell in that order.
- Combine remaining ingredients except parmesan cheese then pour over chicken mixture.
- Sprinkle parmesan cheese on top then bake at 375 for 30 minutes.

49. Chicken And Corn Chowder Recipe

Serving: 4 | Prep: | Cook: | Ready in:

Ingredients

- 6 ears of fresh corn, husked and silks removed (or 1-30 ounce can corn and 1-15 ounce can cream corn)
- 6 slices bacon, chopped
- 8 scallions
- 3 medium potatoes (I use Idaho potatoes)
- 2 tablespoons all-purpose flour
- 3 cups whole milk
- 2 cups chicken stock
- 2 teaspoons Old Bay seasoning
- 1 teaspoon dried parsley flakes
- 1/2 teaspoon dried thyme
- 1/4 teaspoon cayenne pepper
- 1 small can (4 ounces, I believe) chopped green chiles

- 2 cups roasted chicken, shredded (a Rotisserie chicken from the deli works great for this!)
- Salt and pepper, to taste
- handful of grated cheddar, for garnish
- Read more at http://www.bunsinmyoven.com/2011/02/18/corn-and-chicken-chowder/#cf6GtpehP9b78Tlf.99

Direction

- In a large stock pot, fry the bacon pieces until crisp. Remove from the pan, leaving the drippings, and set aside.
- Peel and chop the potatoes into bite sized chunks. Slice the scallions very thin and separate the greens from the whites.
- Place the potatoes and white scallion pieces into the stock pot and cook over medium heat until the scallions have softened, 2 or 3 minutes.
- Sprinkle in the flour and cook, stirring constantly, for about 1 minute.
- Pour in the milk, chicken stock, Old Bay, thyme, parsley, cayenne, salt, and pepper, stirring well. Bring to a boil over medium heat, stirring occasionally.
- Reduce heat to low and simmer for 12-15 minutes or until the potatoes are tender. Add corn (If using fresh corn, cut from the cob with a sharp knife. Use the back of your knife to release the pulp from the cob.), chicken, and green chilies. Cook over low heat until heated through, about 5 minutes. Garnish with scallion greens, bacon, and cheddar cheese.

50. Chicken Brocolli Quiche Recipe

Serving: 6 | Prep: | Cook: 35mins | Ready in:

Ingredients

- 1 can cream of chicken soup
- 1 cup milk
- 6 eggs (NF)

- pinch of cayenne pepper or papricka
- 10 ounces brocolli
- 1 cup shredded cheese
- 2 frozen pie crusts

Direction

- Bake at 450 20-25 minutes.

51. Chicken Enchilada Quiche Recipe

Serving: 8 | Prep: | Cook: 65mins | Ready in:

Ingredients

- 1 Pillsbury(R) refrigerated pie crust, softened as directed on box
- 4 eggs
- 1 cup half-and-half or milk
- 1 1/2 cups canned chicken, drained
- 1 1/2 cups broken tortilla chips
- 2 cups shredded monterey jack cheese
- 1 cup shredded cheddar cheese
- 1 cup Old El Paso(R) Thick 'n chunky salsa
- 1 (4.5 ounce) can Old El Paso(R) Chopped Green Chiles
- 1/2 teaspoon salt
- pepper, to taste (optional)
- sour cream (optional)
- Old El Paso(R) Thick 'n chunky salsa (optional)

Direction

- Heat oven to 350 degrees F. Place pie crust in 9- or 9 1/2-inch glass deep-dish pie pan as directed on box for One-Crust Filled Pie.
- In medium bowl, beat eggs with wire whisk until blended. Beat in half-and-half. Stir in chicken, chips, both cheeses, 1 cup salsa, the green chilies and salt. Pour into crust-lined pan. Sprinkle pepper over top of filling.
- Bake 55 to 65 minutes or until crust is light golden brown and knife inserted in center

comes out clean. Let stand 10 minutes before serving. Cut into wedges. Serve with sour cream and/or salsa.

52. Chicken Olive Cheddar Quiche Recipe

Serving: 6 | Prep: | Cook: 45mins | Ready in:

Ingredients

- piecrust (boughten or homemade)
- 2 c chopped chicken
- 1 c sliced, fresh button mushrooms
- 2-3 green onions, chopped
- 2 T sliced black olives
- 1 clove garlic, minced
- 2 T chopped fresh or 1 tsp. dried basil
- 1/4 tsp. ground red pepper
- vegetable cooking spray
- 1 c shredded Cheddar
- 1 c. half and half
- 4 large eggs
- 1/4 tsp black pepper

Direction

- Carefully place piecrust in 9 inch pie plate. Fold edges under and crimp.
- Bake on lowest rack at 400 for 8 minutes. Cool.
- Sauté chicken and next 6 ingredients in skillet coated with cooking spray over med. heat 5 minutes. Spoon mixture into prepared crust. Sprinkle with cheese.
- Whisk together half and half, eggs, 1/4 tsp. black pepper. Pour over chicken mixture.
- Bake 400 on lowest oven rack for 45 minutes or until set. Let stand 10 minutes. Also delicious served cold.

53. Chicken Taco Quiche

Serving: 0 | Prep: | Cook: |Ready in:

Ingredients

- 2 unbaked pastry shells (9 inches)
- 2 cups cubed cooked chicken
- 2 envelopes taco seasoning, divided
- 2/3 cup salsa
- 2 cups shredded cheddar cheese
- 8 large eggs
- 2 cups half-and-half cream
- 2 tablespoons butter, melted
- 1 can (4 ounces) chopped green chiles
- 1/2 cup sliced ripe olives

Direction

- Line unpricked pastry shells with a double thickness of heavy-duty foil. Bake at 400° for 4 minutes. Remove foil; bake 4 minutes longer.
- In a small bowl, combine chicken and one envelope taco seasoning; spoon into pastry shells. Top with salsa and cheese. In a large bowl, whisk the eggs, cream, butter and remaining taco seasoning. Stir in chiles and olives. Pour over cheese.
- Cover edge of quiches loosely with foil; place on baking sheets. Bake at 400° for 33-35 minutes or until a knife inserted in the center comes out clean. Let stand for 10 minutes before cutting.
- Freeze option: Cover and freeze unbaked quiches. To use, remove from freezer 30 minutes before baking (do not thaw). Preheat oven to 400°. Place quiches on baking sheets; cover edge loosely with foil. Bake as directed, increasing time as necessary for a knife inserted in the center to come out clean.
- Nutrition Facts
- 1 piece: 412 calories, 26g fat (13g saturated fat), 213mg cholesterol, 762mg sodium, 24g carbohydrate (3g sugars, 0 fiber), 18g protein.

54. Chiles Rellenos Quiche

Serving: 4 | Prep: | Cook: 30mins |Ready in:

Ingredients

- Pastry for single-crust pie
- 2 tablespoons cornmeal
- 1-1/2 cups shredded Monterey Jack cheese
- 1 cup shredded cheddar cheese
- 1 can (4 ounces) chopped green chiles
- 3 large eggs
- 3/4 cup sour cream
- 1 tablespoon minced fresh cilantro
- 2 to 4 drops hot pepper sauce, optional

Direction

- In a pie plate, line unpricked crust with a double thickness of heavy-duty foil. Bake at 450° for 8 minutes. Remove foil; bake 5 minutes longer. Cool on a wire rack. Reduce heat to 350°.
- Sprinkle cornmeal over bottom of crust. In a small bowl, combine cheeses; set aside 1/2 cup for topping. Add chiles to remaining cheese mixture; sprinkle into crust.
- In a small bowl, whisk the eggs, sour cream, cilantro and hot pepper sauce if desired. Pour into crust; sprinkle with reserved cheese mixture.
- Bake until a knife inserted in the center comes out clean, 35-40 minutes. Let stand for 5 minutes before cutting.
- Freeze option: Cover and freeze unbaked quiche. To use, remove from freezer 30 minutes before baking (do not thaw). Preheat oven to 350°. Place quiche on a baking sheet; cover edge loosely with foil. Bake as directed, increasing time as necessary for a knife inserted in the center to come out clean.
- Nutrition Facts
- 1 slice: 444 calories, 31g fat (18g saturated fat), 178mg cholesterol, 520mg sodium, 23g carbohydrate (3g sugars, 1g fiber), 17g protein.

55. Chili Con Queso BitesQuiche Recipe

Serving: 8 | Prep: | Cook: 12mins |Ready in:

Ingredients

- 4 eggs
- 1/2 cup Pace® Picante Sauce
- 1/4 cup all-purpose flour
- 2 teaspoons chili powder
- 1 1/2 cups shredded cheddar cheese
- 1 green onion, chopped

Direction

- Heat the oven to 400 degrees F. Lightly grease 24 (3-inch) muffin-pan cups.
- Beat the eggs, picante sauce, flour and chili powder in a medium bowl with a fork or whisk. Stir in the cheese and onion.
- Spoon about 1 tablespoon cheese mixture into each muffin-pan cup. Bake for 10 minutes or until the bites are golden brown. Serve warm or at room temperature with additional picante sauce

56. Cindys Awesomely Yummy Quiche Recipe

Serving: 8 | Prep: | Cook: 15mins |Ready in:

Ingredients

- 4 large eggs
- 1/2 cup sour cream
- 1 package frozen broccoli florets, thawed and drained well (Press hard in colander to remove water; then use a paper towel to absorb all of the excess water after you've drained broccoli ~ you want this to be relatively dry before you combine with the egg mixture.
- 1 uncooked, deep dish pie crust, Pillsbury a must here
- 1 pound swiss cheese, grated

- Note: You can substitute spinach for the broccoli; just follow the same rule for draining the water out of it.

Direction

- Preheat oven to 350.
- Beat eggs ~ use hand whisk or mixer.
- Add sour cream and mix well.
- Stir in broccoli and cheese, then pour into unbaked pie crust.
- Bake for about 15-20 minutes or until firm and golden brown on top. DO NOT OVERCOOK!
- Serve hot with crispy bacon or sage sausage and white grapes on the side. Yummy!

57. Coconut Milk Rice Recipe

Serving: 0 | Prep: | Cook: 25mins |Ready in:

Ingredients

- long grained rice - 2cups
- coconutmilk   - 2 cups
- onion - 2
- green chillies - 3
- garlic flakes - 12
- cinnamon stick - 2
- cardamon - 3
- cloves - 4
- cashew nuts - 10
- ghee(clarified butter) - 4 tbl
- lemon juice - few drops(optional)
- salt - to taste

Direction

- Soak rice in water for half an hour and drain the water completely.
- Cut the onion and chillies lengthwise.
- Add water to the coconut milk and make it as four cups.
- In a cooking pot add ghee, cinnamon stick, cardamom and cloves and fry.

- Add cashew nuts and garlic and fry till it turn brown.
- Now add onion and chillies and fry till the onion turns transparent.
- Add the rice to it and stir gently till the rice get heated.
- Now add the coconut milk, salt and lemon juice.
- Cook till the water is absorbed.
- Serve hot with spicy gravy and potato chips.

58. Corn Tortilla Quiche Recipe

Serving: 6 | Prep: | Cook: 45mins | Ready in:

Ingredients

- 3/4 lb bulk pork sausage
- 5 (6") corn tortillas
- 1 c shredded Monteray Jack cheese
- 1 c shredded cheddar cheese
- 1/4 c canned chopped green chilies
- 6 eggs,beaten
- 1/2 c whipping cream
- 1/2 c small curd cottage cheese
- 1/2 tsp chili powder
- 1/4 c minced fresh cilantro or parsley

Direction

- In skillet, cook sausage till no longer pink; drain. Place four tortillas in a greased 9" pie plate, overlapping and extending 1/2" beyond rim Place remaining tortilla in the center. Layer with sausage, Monterey Jack and cheddar cheeses and chilies. Combine eggs, cream, cottage cheese and chili powder; slowly pour over chilies. Bake at 350 degrees for 45 mins or till center is set and puffed. Sprinkle with cilantro. Cut in wedges

59. Corned Beef Quiche Recipe

Serving: 8 | Prep: | Cook: 40mins | Ready in:

Ingredients

- 12 oz corned beef Finely diced
- 1 Unbaked pie shell
- 3/4 c Finely Diced onion Sauteed
- 3/4 c sliced mushrooms Sauteed
- 1/2 c Swiss or cheddar cheese Grated
- 4 lg eggs
- 2 tbsp flour
- 1 1/4 c milk
- 1/4 tsp nutmeg Grated
- 1/4 tsp pepper salt To Taste

Direction

- Layer onion, mushrooms, HEREFORD Corned Beef, and cheese in pastry shell.
- Beat eggs, flour, and milk together until well mixed; add seasonings. (Omit salt if cheddar cheese is used.)
- Pour mixture over ingredients in pie shell. Bake at 350 F (180 C) for 40 minutes or until knife inserted in center comes out clean.
- Serve hot or warm.

60. Cousin Lisas Quiche Recipe

Serving: 4 | Prep: | Cook: 30mins | Ready in:

Ingredients

- 2 T butter
- small onion diced finely
- mushrooms sliced
- 2 cups baby spinach (uncooked)
- cooked ham diced
- 2 T flour
- 1 t salt
- 1/2 t pepper
- 1 cup milk
- 3 beaten eggs

- 1 cup cheddar cheese grated
- pie crust... optional. (I mostly make it without.)

Direction

- Melt butter and sauté mushrooms and onions.
- Stir in flour, salt and pepper.
- Add milk and cook until thickened.
- Remove from heat and add eggs, spinach, ham and cheese.
- Pour into greased pie plate and bake at 375 for 30 minutes.
- Let stand 10 minutes before serving.
- If you want a crust, put crust in pie plate, layer cheese on the bottom and then pour egg mixture on and bake the same way.

61. Crab & Swiss Cheese Crustless Quiche Recipe

Serving: 8 | Prep: | Cook: 40mins | Ready in:

Ingredients

- 2 eggs, lightly beaten
- 1/2 cup milk
- 1/2 cup mayonnaise
- 1 teaspoon cornstarch
- 1/2 pound imitation crab meat, flaked
- 1 1/2 cups shredded swiss cheese

Direction

- Preheat oven to 350 degrees. In a bowl, mix together eggs, milk, mayonnaise and cornstarch, mix in the crab and cheese. Pour into dish, which has been sprayed with cooking spray.
- Bake in preheated oven until a knife inserted into center of the quiche comes out clean about 40 minutes!

62. Crab And Spinach Quiche Recipe

Serving: 6 | Prep: | Cook: 60mins | Ready in:

Ingredients

- Pastry crust, ready-made or make your own (see below)
- 2 cups shredded swiss cheese
- 1/2 cup grated parmesan cheese
- 2 Tbsp all-purpose flour
- 1 tsp paprika or cayenne
- 1/4 tsp salt
- 1 41/2 oz can white crab
- 1 can spinach , drained and chopped OR1 small package frozen spinach, defrosted, drained and chopped OR 6oz fresh spinach, chopped
- 1/2 cup milk
- 4 eggs, lightly beaten
- For pastry dough:
- 1 cup all-purpose flour
- 1/2 tsp salt
- 1/3 cup shortening
- 2-3 Tbsp cold water
- 1 tsp vinegar

Direction

- Preheat oven to 425F.
- To make pastry:
- Combine flour and salt in a mixing bowl.
- Cut in shortening with 2 knives or a pastry cutter until mixture is the consistency of cornmeal.
- Add vinegar and then add water, 1 Tbsp. at a time until mixture is moist.
- Turn out onto floured board and roll out to the size of quiche pan plus 1 inch extra for fluting.
- Drape pastry over quiche pan and gently press into place.
- Flute the edges using your forefingers and thumbs, moving around the edge until completed.
- Do not bake.
- Filling:

- In a small bowl toss the Swiss cheese, Parmesan cheese, flour, salt and paprika until well blended.
- In a large bowl mix together the eggs and milk with a whisk
- Add the crab and spinach and mix well.
- Fold the cheese mixture into the egg, crab and spinach mixture and mix well.
- Pour the completed mixture into the unbaked pastry shell.
- Bake at 425F for 15 minutes (do not open oven door during this time), then reduce heat to 350F and bake for 45 minutes or until top of quiche is firm and starting to brown.
- Serve with a nice green salad.

63. Crab Quiche Recipe

Serving: 8 | Prep: | Cook: 35mins | Ready in:

Ingredients

- 1 unbaked pastry shell (9 inches)
- 1 cup shredded swiss cheese, divided (4 ounces)
- 1/2 cup chopped sweet red pepper
- 1/4 cup chopped green onions
- 1 tablespoon butter
- 3 eggs
- 1 1/2 cups half and half cream
- 1/2 teaspoon salt
- 1/4 teaspoon pepper
- 3/4 cup flaked imitation crabmeat, chopped

Direction

- Line unpricked pastry shell with a double thickness of heavy duty foil.
- Bake at 450 degrees for 5 minutes; remove foil and bake 5 minutes longer.
- Immediately sprinkle 1/2 cup cheese over crust.
- Reduce heat to 375 degrees.
- In a skillet sauté red pepper and onions in butter until tender.

- In a large bowl, whisk the eggs, cream, salt and pepper.
- Stir in the crab and red pepper mixture.
- Pour into crust.
- Bake for 30 to 35 minutes or until knife inserted near the center comes out clean.
- Let stand for 15 minutes before cutting.
- 6 to 8 servings.

64. Crab Quiche Recipe

Serving: 6 | Prep: | Cook: 60mins | Ready in:

Ingredients

- 8 ounces crabmeat (fresh or from flavor pouches), drain excess liquid
- 1/2 cup half & half
- 1/4 cup sliced green onion
- 1 (10 3/4-oz) can cream of chicken soup
- 4 large eggs
- 2 cups grated cheddar cheese
- 1 (9-in) deep dish pie shell, thawed

Direction

- Preheat oven to 350 degrees.
- In a large mixing bowl, combine all ingredients and pour into pie shell.
- Bake for 1 hour.
- Cool for 20 minutes so the quiche can set up.

65. Crabmeat Quiche Recipe

Serving: 6 | Prep: | Cook: 30mins | Ready in:

Ingredients

- 3 tablespoons butter
- 2 tablespoons chopped green onion
- 3 tablespoons chopped red bell pepper
- 1 cup crabmeat, drained and flaked
- salt and pepper to taste

- 2 tablespoons white wine
- 3 eggs, beaten
- 1 cup half-and-half cream
- 1 (9 inch) pie shell, partially baked
- 1/2 cup shredded swiss cheese

Direction

- Preheat oven to 375 degrees F (190 degrees C).
- Heat butter in a large skillet over medium heat. Sauté green onion and red bell pepper until soft. Stir in crabmeat, and season with salt and pepper. Add wine, and cook for 1 minute. Remove from heat, and allow to cool.
- In a large bowl, beat eggs until light. Whisk in half-and-half, and crab mixture. Pour into pie crust, and sprinkle with Swiss cheese.
- Bake in preheated oven for 25 to 30 minutes, or until puffed and golden brown.

66. Crouton Quiche Recipe

Serving: 6 | Prep: | Cook: 30mins | Ready in:

Ingredients

- 1 box of croutons for salad (I like garlic.herb)
- 2 eggs
- 1 1/2 cup milk
- 1/2 to 1 cup cup shredded favoritwe cheese
- some chopped cooked broccoli and chopped ham if desired
- salt and pepper to taste

Direction

- Grease a square pan (9 x 9 inch) or Pyrex pie dish.
- Mix eggs, milk, cheese and salt and pepper (add a bit of broccoli or chopped ham opt).
- Place croutons in a square pan.
- Spread evenly.
- Pour on the milk mixture. Make sure croutons are covered with liquid
- Top with additional cheese if desired.

- Bake in a 350F preheated oven until golden and set

67. Crustless Artichoke And Spinach Mini Quiche Recipe

Serving: 12 | Prep: | Cook: 30mins | Ready in:

Ingredients

- 10 oz frozen chopped spinach
- 1 cup grated mozzarella
- 3 eggs
- 1 lb ricotta
- 1 small chopped onion
- 1 clove garlic
- 1 tsp salt
- 2 tbsp olive oil
- 1 can artichokes

Direction

- 1. Preheat oven to 350 degrees.
- 2. Cook spinach until wilted. Squeeze dry.
- 3. Mix eggs, ricotta, mozzarella, onions, oil, artichokes and spinach together.
- 4. Bake in muffins for 20 minutes. (If you want to put it all in a spring form, bake for 40 minutes).

68. Crustless Bacon Quiche Recipe

Serving: 12 | Prep: | Cook: 45mins | Ready in:

Ingredients

- 12 slices bacon
- 2 tbsp creamery butter
- 1 onion, chopped
- 1 leek, chopped
- 1 red bell pepper, chopped
- 3 cloves garlic, minced

- 1 10-oz pkg frozen, chopped spinach, thawed
- 2 cups shredded cheddar cheese
- 2 cups shredded havarti cheese
- 12 eggs
- 1/2 cup light cream
- 1 tsp dried thyme leaves
- 1/2 tsp salt
- 1/8 tsp white pepper
- 1/4 cup grated parmesan cheese

Direction

- Preheat oven to 350*F.
- Grease or spray a 9"x13" glass baking pan; set aside.
- In large skillet, cook bacon until crisp.
- HINT: for less fat, cook the bacon in the microwave between paper towelling; the towels absorb the grease.
- Crumble bacon; set aside.
- Reserve 1 tbsp. bacon drippings.
- Place drippings into skillet with 1 tbsp. creamery butter.
- Add garlic & leek to skillet.
- Cook & stir for 5 minutes.
- Add bell peppers & garlic; cook another 2 minutes.
- Drain spinach well; add to skillet.
- Remove from heat.
- Place veggie mixture into baking dish.
- Top with crumbled bacon.
- Layer cheddar & Havarti on top.
- In large bowl, beat the eggs with the cream, thyme, salt, and pepper, until smooth.
- Pour into baking dish, over contents.
- Sprinkle with Parmesan cheese.
- Bake 35-45 minutes, until egg mixture is set and the top is beginning to brown.
- Let stand 5 minutes to firm up, then serve.

69. Crustless Broccoli N Cheddar Mini Quiches Recipe

Serving: 12 | Prep: | Cook: 23mins | Ready in:

Ingredients

- :
- :
- 1 can (12 fl. oz.) NESTLÉ® CARNATION® Evaporated milk
- 3 large eggs, beaten
- 2 tablespoons all-purpose flour
- 1/4 teaspoon salt
- 1/4 teaspoon ground black pepper
- 2 cups (8 oz.) shredded mild or sharp cheddar cheese
- 2 cups chopped, frozen broccoli, thawed and drained
- 1/2 cup chopped red bell pepper

Direction

- COOKING TIME 15 MINUTES
- ----
- PREHEAT oven to 350° F.
- Grease and lightly flour twelve 2 1/2-inch muffin cups.
- WHISK evaporated milk, eggs, flour, salt and black pepper in medium bowl until blended.
- Stir in cheese, broccoli and bell pepper. Spoon 1/4 to 1/3 cup of mixture into each prepared muffin cup, filling almost to rim.
- Stir mixture frequently to evenly distribute ingredients.
- BAKE for 23 to 28 minutes or until knife inserted near centers comes out clean and tops are lightly browned.
- Cool in pans for 15 minutes.
- Run knife or small, flat spatula around inside edges of muffin cups. Carefully remove quiches.

70. Crustless Chicken, Cheese, Sun Dried Tomatoes,onions, Peppers Recipe

Serving: 8 | Prep: | Cook: 30mins | Ready in:

Ingredients

- 1 onion sliced
- 1-2 cups chicken breast diced
- 6 eggs
- 3 cups shredded cheese
- 1/4 teaspoon salt
- 1/8 teaspoon pepper
- Sun dried tomatoes - as much as you like
- diced yellow pepper - 1/4 cup

Direction

- 1. Preheat oven to 350 degrees f and spray a quiche dish with non-stick cooking spray.
- 2. In a bowl crack the eggs and beat add the cheese, onion, sun dried tomatoes, pepper salt and pepper.
- 3. Mix well together and then place in the quiche dish and bake for about 30 minutes or until firm to touch and golden brown.

71. Crustless Crab Quiche With Spring Vegetables Recipe

Serving: 6 | Prep: | Cook: 40mins | Ready in:

Ingredients

- 1-1/2 cups crabmeat
- 3/4 cup roasted hazelnuts coarsely chopped
- 1-1/2 cups grated gruyere cheese
- 1-1/2 cups asparagus sliced diagonally
- 2 tablespoons sweet white onion diced
- 4 eggs
- 2-2/3 cups milk
- 1-1/2 cups baking mix
- 5 whole asparagus spears for top garnish

Direction

- Heat oven to 400.
- Coat a quiche dish with non-stick cooking spray.
- Reserve 1/4 cup of hazelnuts for garnish.

- Layer crab, 1/2 cup nuts, cheese and vegetables in baking dish.
- In separate mixing bowl whisk together eggs and milk until incorporated.
- Batter will be somewhat lumpy.
- Pour over layered ingredients in baking dish.
- Bake 40 minutes or until golden brown.
- Allow to stand 5 minutes before serving.
- Blanch reserved asparagus for 8 minutes in uncovered pot.
- Drain on paper towels.
- When quiche is removed from oven garnish with asparagus.
- Sprinkle hazelnuts over all.
- To give asparagus a shiny appearance brush very lightly with vegetable oil.

72. Crustless Four Cheese Quiche Recipe

Serving: 8 | Prep: | Cook: 40mins | Ready in:

Ingredients

- * 1/4 cup butter
- * 1/4 cup all-purpose flour
- * 3/4 cup milk
- * 1-1/4 cups 4% cottage cheese
- * 1/2 teaspoon baking powder
- * 1/2 teaspoon ground mustard
- * 1/4 teaspoon salt
- * 5 eggs
- * 2 packages (3 ounces each) cream cheese, cubed
- * 1/2 pound Jarlsberg or swiss cheese, shredded
- * 1/4 cup grated parmesan cheese

Direction

- In a small saucepan, melt butter. Stir in flour until smooth; gradually add milk. Bring to a boil; cook and stir for 2 minutes or until thickened and bubbly. Remove from the heat; cool for 15 minutes.

- Meanwhile, in a small bowl, combine the cottage cheese, baking powder, mustard and salt. In a large bowl, beat eggs. Slowly beat in the cream cheese, cottage cheese mixture and white sauce until smooth. Fold in the Jarlsberg and Parmesan.
- Pour into a greased 9-in. pie plate. Bake at 350° for 35-40 minutes or until a knife inserted near the center comes out clean. Let stand for 5 minutes before cutting. Serve warm. Refrigerate leftovers. Yield: 6 servings.

73. Crustless Garden Veggie Quiche Recipe

Serving: 6 | Prep: | Cook: 25mins | Ready in:

Ingredients

- 1 tablespoon olive oil
- 1 cup sliced mushrooms
- 1/2 med. zucchini, halved lengthwise and sliced
- 1/2 small onion, diced
- 1/4 cup red bell pepper, diced
- 1/3 cup shredded carrots
- 2 cloves garlic, crushed
- 1 teaspoon salt
- 5 eggs
- 1/2 cup ricotta cheese
- 1/3 cup parmesan cheese
- 1/3 cup grated parmesan cheese

Direction

- Heat olive oil in medium size pan.
- Add veggies, garlic, and salt and sauté until soft.
- While veggies are cooling a little, mix together eggs, ricotta, and parmesan until fully combined.
- Stir veggies into egg mixture and pour into pie plate.
- Cook at 350 for 25-30 minutes.
- Enjoy!

- *Also great topped with fresh tomato slices

74. Crustless Leek And Gruyere Quiche Recipe

Serving: 6 | Prep: | Cook: 40mins | Ready in:

Ingredients

- 2 large leeks, cleaned and sliced (white and pale green parts)
- 1 onion, sliced finely
- 2 tablespoons olive oil
- 4 eggs
- 1/2 cup coffee cream (5%)
- 1 cup light Gruyère (15%), grated
- 1/8 teaspoon ground nutmeg
- 1 pinch smoky paprika (pimenton de la vera)
- 1 tablespoon Dijon mustard
- Big pinch dry thyme
- salt and pepper to taste
- 2 tablespoons flour

Direction

- Grease a 9" pie pan (and find a larger pan to serve as water bath).
- Sauté leeks and onion with oil in a non-stick pan until tender. Add salt and pepper.
- Meanwhile, beat together eggs, cream, gruyere, flour, herbs and seasonings until well mixed.
- Pour into pie pan.
- Add sautéed vegetables.
- Sprinkle some extra grated cheese on top.
- Place in larger pan and slide into oven.
- Pour boiling water into the larger pan so the quiche sits halfway up in the water.
- Bake in the oven at 375 degrees F for 35 to 40 minutes, or until the top is light brown.
- Remove from oven, lift out of water pan, and let cool on a rack.
- Serve warm or cool.

75. Crustless Pierogi Quiche Recipe

Serving: 6 | Prep: | Cook: 60mins | Ready in:

Ingredients

- 1 (16-ounce) box Mrs. T's potato and cheddar pierogis (I use mini)
- 1 Tbsp. butter or margarine
- 1 small red bell pepper, thinly sliced
- 1 cup mushrooms, sliced
- 3 cups baby spinach
- 2 scallions, sliced
- 1 1/2 cups milk
- 3 large eggs
- 3/4 tsp. salt
- 1/4 tsp. ground black pepper
- 1 cup shredded Asiago cheese (can customize with different cheeses if desired)
- *** I add 4 slices crumbled crisp bacon at final step of mixing all together.

Direction

- Preheat oven to 350°F.
- Boil pierogies as box directs.
- Melt butter in 12-inch skillet over medium heat; add red pepper slices and mushrooms. Cook, stirring frequently, about 5 minutes or until just tender. Remove to bowl with slotted spoon. Add spinach and scallions to drippings remaining in skillet; cook about 3 minutes or until just wilted. Remove to bowl with vegetables.
- Grease a 3-quart casserole dish. Beat milk, eggs, salt and pepper in large bowl, until well mixed. Add vegetables, cheese and cooked pierogies. Pour mixture into prepared casserole dish. Bake 40 minutes, or until mixture is puffed and golden.

76. Crustless Quiche Recipe

Serving: 4 | Prep: | Cook: 50mins | Ready in:

Ingredients

- 1 tablespoon butter
- 1 medium onion or leek
- 1 potato or kumera, grated
- 1 carrot, grated
- 2 zucchini, grated
- 2 tablespoons plain flour
- 1/2 cup chopped fresh parsley
- 4 eggs, lightly beaten
- 300g sour cream
- 1/2 cup shredded parmesan
- 1 teaspoon salt
- 1/2 teaspoon nutmeg or allspice

Direction

- Preheat oven to 180 degrees C.
- Melt butter in a small frying pan, add onion, and stir over medium heat for 2 minutes until onion is soft.
- In a large bowl combine the grated vegetables and parsley with the flour and cheese.
- Add the cooked onion, sour cream and eggs and mix well.
- Pour the mixture into a greased pie dish and bake in a pre-heated oven for 45 minutes.

77. Crustless Quiche Shrimp Bacon Mushroom Recipe

Serving: 8 | Prep: | Cook: 50mins | Ready in:

Ingredients

- 8 large eggs
- 1 cup regular mayo
- 1/2 to 1 cup half and half, or soy milk, depending on
- desired consistency
- 2 cups swiss cheese grated

- my favorite:
- 6 oz lean turkey bacon, cooked and crumbled
- 8 oz small fresh or frozen shrimp
- 8 oz sliced bella mushrooms
- 2 garlic cloves crushed
- seasonings as desired - i don't add salt or pepper
- i've used combinations of spinach, onions, broccoli, mushrooms
- lean beef, shrimp, sausage, kielbasa
- a kids favorite is lean beef with cheddar
- use your imagination and make it different every time.

Direction

- Cook bacon in skillet, cool and crumble.
- Sauté shrimp in olive oil and crushed garlic, set aside.
- Sauté mushrooms - using fresh uncooked causes too much.
- Water in the quiche.
- In a large bowl, hand whip the eggs.
- With a spatula mix in the mayo until smooth.
- Add the cheese and mix.
- 9 inch quiche dish, 350 F 45-50 minutes until raised, golden brown, with splits across the top.
- Starting with the liquid mix, layer the ingredients, and top with a bit of cheese.

78. Crustless Spinach And Feta Quiche Recipe

Serving: 0 | Prep: | Cook: 1hours | Ready in:

Ingredients

- 1 dozen eggs
- 1/2 cup soy or cows milk
- 1 cup grated tasty cheese
- 1 cup of feta cubes
- 2 cups of steamed spinach
- 2 vegetable stock cubes

- 1 tbsp chives
- 1 tomato for decoration, optional

Direction

- Blend eggs, milk and stock cubes.
- Stir in remaining ingredients.
- Pour into suitably sized baking dish.
- Bake at a medium temperature 160 -180C for 40 -50 minutes.
- Serve with crusty bread and a tossed salad.

79. Crustless Spinach Quiche

Serving: 6 | Prep: | Cook: 15mins | Ready in:

Ingredients

- 1 cup chopped onion
- 1 cup sliced fresh mushrooms
- 1 tablespoon vegetable oil
- 1 package (10 ounces) frozen chopped spinach, thawed and well drained
- 2/3 cup finely chopped fully cooked ham
- 5 large eggs
- 3 cups shredded Muenster or Monterey Jack cheese
- 1/8 teaspoon pepper

Direction

- In a large skillet, saute onion and mushrooms in oil until tender. Add spinach and ham; cook and stir until the excess moisture is evaporated. Cool slightly. Beat eggs; add cheese and mix well. Stir in spinach mixture and pepper; blend well. Spread evenly into a greased 9-in. pie plate or quiche dish. Bake at 350° for 40-45 minutes or until a knife inserted in center comes out clean.
- Tips
- To ensure perfectly cooked quiche, start checking early to see whether it's done. Baking times are great guidelines, but because every oven heats differently, we recommend taking

an early look, especially for cakes, cookies, muffins and delicate egg-based dishes.

- For cheese that's extra melty, shred or grate it yourself.
- Check out 10 of our best quiche recipes.
- Nutrition Facts
- 1 piece: 251 calories, 18g fat (10g saturated fat), 164mg cholesterol, 480mg sodium, 4g carbohydrate (2g sugars, 1g fiber), 18g protein.

80. Crustless Spinach Quiche Recipe

Serving: 6 | Prep: | Cook: 30mins | Ready in:

Ingredients

- 1 tablespoon vegetable oil
- 1 onion, chopped
- 1 (10 ounce) package frozen chopped spinach, thawed and drained
- 5 eggs, beaten
- 3 cups shredded muenster cheese
- 1/4 teaspoon salt
- 1/8 teaspoon ground black pepper

Direction

- Preheat oven to 350 degrees F (175 degrees C). Lightly grease a 9 inch pie pan.
- Heat oil in a large skillet over medium-high heat.
- Add onions and cook, stirring occasionally, until onions are soft.
- Stir in spinach and continue cooking until excess moisture has evaporated.
- In a large bowl, combine eggs, cheese, salt and pepper.
- Add spinach mixture and stir to blend.
- Scoop into prepared pie pan.
- Bake in preheated oven until eggs have set, about 30 minutes. Let cool for 10 minutes before serving.

81. Crustless Vegetables Mini Quiches Recipe

Serving: 48 | Prep: | Cook: 45mins | Ready in:

Ingredients

- 1/2 cup Hellmans mayonnaise
- 6 tablespoons all purpose flour
- 2 cups grated cheese (mild, medium, old or extra old to your taste)
- 1 cup milk
- 5 eggs
- 1 small onion, diced
- 1 cup fresh brocoli, finely chopped (or frozen)
- 1 cup fresh cauliflower, coarsely chopped (or frozen)
- 1 small zucchini, coarsely chopped OR 1 cup mushrooms, coarsely chopped or any other vegetable you have on hand
- salt and pepper to taste
- 1/2 cup parmesan cheese

Direction

- In the food processor, mix the mayonnaise and the flour.
- Add all the other ingredients EXCEPT the parmesan cheese. Process until you obtain finely chopped vegetables (not too finely chopped, you want vegetable chunks.
- Pour this mixture in a 12 mini-muffins pan well oiled.
- Put the parmesan cheese on top of each mini-quiche.
- Place in 375 degrees oven for 30 minutes then lower the oven to 350 degrees and continue cooking for an additional 15 minutes.
- Check often in the last 15 minutes so they do not get overcooked.
- Serve immediately as appetizers.
- They may be frozen and re-heated.
- Variations: You may also add 1 cup of crab meat, ham or other meat of your choice.

82. Crustless Zuchinni Quiche Recipe

Serving: 6 | Prep: | Cook: 32mins | Ready in:

Ingredients

- 2 medium size zuchinni {shredded{6 cups}
- 2 cups swiss cheese coarsley shredded
- 4 eggs
- 1 cup buttermilk baking mix
- 1/4 cup salad oil
- 1/2 tsp. salt
- 1/4 tsp. italian seasoning
- Preheat oven to 400 degrees
- Grease 9 inch Pie Plate

Direction

- In large bowl with fork or wire whisk mix Zucchini, cheese, eggs, buttermilk baking mix, salad oil, salt and Italian seasoning until well blended.
- Pour mixture into prepared pie plate.
- Bake quiche 30-35 minutes until golden brown and knife inserted comes out clean.

83. Darianas Quiche Lorraine Recipe

Serving: 6 | Prep: | Cook: 60mins | Ready in:

Ingredients

- pastry for single-crust pie
- 8 slices bacon
- 1 medium onion, thinly sliced
- 4 beaten eggs
- 1 cup half-and-half or light cream
- 1 cup milk
- 1/4 teaspoon salt
- Dash ground nutmeg
- 1-1/2 cups shredded swiss cheese (6 ounces)
- 1 tablespoon all-purpose flour
- tomato wedges
- fresh parsley

Direction

- Prepare Pastry for Single-Crust Pie. Line the unpricked pastry shell with a double thickness of heavy duty foil. Bake in a 450 degrees F oven for 8 minutes. Remove foil. Bake for 4 to 5 minutes more or until pastry is set and dry. Remove from oven. Reduce oven temperature to 325 degrees F. (Pie shell should still be hot when filling is added; do not partially bake pastry shell ahead of time.)
- Meanwhile, in a large skillet cook bacon until crisp. Drain, reserving 2 tablespoons drippings. Crumble bacon finely; set aside. Cook sliced onion in reserved drippings over medium heat until tender but not brown; drain.
- In a medium mixing bowl stir together the eggs, half-and-half, milk, salt, and nutmeg. Stir in the crumbled bacon and onion. Toss together shredded cheese and flour. Add to egg mixture; mix well.
- Pour egg mixture into the hot, baked pastry shell. Bake in the 325 degrees F oven for 50 to 60 minutes or until a knife inserted near the center comes out clean. If necessary, cover edge of crust with foil to prevent overbrowning. Let stand 10 minutes. Garnish with tomatoes and parsley before serving. Makes 6 servings.
- Pastry for Single-Crust Pie: In a medium bowl stir together -1/4 cups all-purpose flour and 1/4 teaspoon salt. Using a pastry blender, cut in 1/3 cup shortening until pieces are pea-size. Sprinkle 1 tablespoon of cold water over part of the flour mixture; gently toss with a fork. Push moistened dough to the side of the bowl. Repeat moistening flour mixture, 1 tablespoon at a time, until all is moistened (use 4 or 5 tablespoons total). Form dough into a ball. On a lightly floured surface, use your hands to slightly flatten dough. Roll dough from center to edges into a circle about 12 inches in

diameter. To transfer pastry, wrap it around the rolling pin. Unroll pastry into a 9-inch pie plate. Ease pastry into pie plate, being careful not to stretch pastry. Trim pastry to 1/2 inch beyond edge of pie plate. Fold under extra pastry. Crimp edge as desired. Do not prick pastry. Bake as directed.

84. Deep Dish Ham Quiche With Herb And Asparagus Salad Recipe

Serving: 8 | Prep: | Cook: 120mins | Ready in:

Ingredients

- Pastry:
- 2 cups all-purpose flour, plus more for dusting
- 1 teaspoon salt
- 1/4 teaspoon sugar
- 3/4 cup (11/2 sticks) unsalted butter, cold and cut into small chunks
- 1 large egg yolk
- 3 tablespoons ice water, plus more if needed.
- ~
- Filling:
- 3 tablespoons extra-virgin-olive oil
- 2 large vidalia onions, sliced
- 3/4 pound smoked ham, cubed
- 8 large eggs
- 1 quart heavy cream
- kosher salt and freshly ground black pepper
- ~
- Salad:
- 2 bunches asparagus (about 1 pound each), stems trimmed
- 4 ounces Parmesan, shaved with a peeler
- 2 handfuls fresh flat-leaf parsley, hand-torn
- 1 handful fresh mint, hand-torn
- 1 handful fresh dill, hand-torn
- extra-virgin olive oil
- 1/2 lemon, juiced
- kosher salt and freshly ground black pepper

Direction

- To make the pastry:
- Combine the flour, salt, and sugar in a large mixing bowl.
- Add the butter and mix with a pastry blender or your hands until the mixture resembles coarse crumbs.
- Beat the egg yolk and ice water in a small bowl to blend, add it to the pastry.
- Work it in to bind the dough until it holds together without being too wet or sticky.
- Squeeze a small amount together, if it is crumbly, add more ice water, 1 tablespoon at a time.
- Form the dough into a disk and wrap in plastic wrap; refrigerate for at least 30 minutes.
- Sprinkle the counter and a rolling pin lightly with flour.
- Roll the dough out into a 14-inch circle about 1/4-inch thick.
- Carefully roll the dough up onto the pin (this may take a little practice) and lay it inside a 9-inch springform pan.
- Press the dough firmly into the bottom and sides so it fits tightly; trim the excess dough around the rim.
- Place the pan on a sturdy cookie sheet so it will be easier to move in and out of the oven, this quiche is pretty heavy.
- Preheat the oven to 375 degrees F.
- ~
- To make the filling:
- Heat a skillet over medium-low heat, coat the pan with oil, and add the onions.
- Slowly cook the onions, stirring, until they caramelize and release their natural sugars.
- Add a couple of tablespoons of water to help the onions break down, if needed.
- Toss in the ham, cook, stirring, for about 10 minutes to get some color on it.
- Remove from heat. In a large bowl, beat the eggs until frothy, pour in the cream; season with salt and pepper.
- Arrange the caramelized onions and ham over the bottom of the crust and carefully pour in

the cream and egg mixture; the filling should be about 1-inch from the top of the pan.

- Cover loosely with foil and bake for 1 hour and 30 minutes.
- Remove the foil and continue to bake for 15 minutes or until the quiche is set, puffy, and jiggles slightly.
- Remove to a wire rack and let cool for 30 minutes.
- In the meantime make the asparagus salad.
- ~
- To make the asparagus salad:
- In a large pot of boiling salted water, blanch the asparagus for 4 minutes, or until they are just crisp-tender.
- Drain the asparagus, transfer to a bowl of ice water to stop the cooking, and drain well.
- Slice the asparagus into 1/2-inch pieces and put them in a mixing bowl.
- Add the Parmesan and herbs, drizzle the herb and asparagus salad with olive oil, a squeeze of lemon juice, season with salt and pepper.
- Toss gently to combine.
- ~
- Loosen the quiche from the sides of the pan by running a thin metal spatula around the inside rim.
- Carefully unmold the ring, and transfer the quiche (with the bottom base) to a serving plate.
- Cut it into wedges, drizzle with a little olive oil, and a few turns of freshly ground black pepper.
- Garnish with the asparagus salad on top.
- ~~~~~~~~~~~~~~~~~~~~~~~~~~~~~~~~~~~ ~~~~~~~~~~~
- Others Changes, by that I mean not me, I have yet to make this good looking quiche:
- Added some chopped red pepper to the quiche, and a splash of balsamic vinegar to the onions as they were caramelizing.
- The only fresh herb on hand for the salad was dill, so I added in some mixed greens as well.
- I already had some pie crust in the freezer from the last batch I made, so I used that. Whenever I make pie crust I make a double

batch and freeze half if I am only making a single crust pie.

- ~~~~~~~~~~~~~~~~~~~~~~~~~~~~~~~~~~~ ~~~~~~~~~~~
- The only change I am thinking of making to this is to use tiny single serving pans so I can make it look this good on all of the plates!!!! Erma

85. Easy Ham And Cheese Quiche Recipe

Serving: 12 | Prep: | Cook: 35mins | Ready in:

Ingredients

- 2 (9 inch) (pie) pastry shells
- 2 cups diced fully cooked ham
- 2 cups shredded sharp cheddar cheese
- 2 teaspoons fresh minced onion
- 4 eggs
- 2 cups half-and-half cream
- 1/2 teaspoon salt
- 1/4 teaspoon pepper

Direction

- Line unpricked pastry shells with a double thickness of heavy-duty foil.
- Bake at 400 degrees F for 5 minutes.
- Remove foil; bake 5 minutes longer.
- Divide ham, cheese and onion between the shells. In a bowl, whisk eggs, cream, salt and pepper.
- Pour into shells, cover edges with foil and bake at 400 degrees F for 35-40 minutes or until a knife inserted near the center comes out clean.
- Let stand for 5-10 minutes before cutting.

86. Easy Impossible One Dish Quiche Recipe

Serving: 8 | Prep: | Cook: 30mins | Ready in:

Ingredients

- 12 eggs
- 3 table spoons of self raising flour
- 1 cup of milk or cream
- salt and pepper
- Can pink salmon
- 1 large red onion
- Fresh dill
- butter

Direction

- Put a butter greased quiche dish in the fridge, this isn't essential if you don't have the time, but it does make a difference if you do. Pre heat the oven to 200 degrees.
- Take your chilled quiche dish add the 12 eggs, mix the flour and milk together and then mix into the eggs until evenly mixed.
- Finely dice the onion, drain the salmon and roughly chop the dill, distribute them evenly into the egg mix, no need to stir.
- Bake until golden brown, and almost firm. Do remember that the eggs will continue to cook after they have left the oven. Sit for 10 min then serve.
- This is easily adapted to your favourite quiche ingredients; I have just used salmon and dill because it's my personal favourite.

87. Easy Phyllo Crab Quiche Recipe

Serving: 8 | Prep: | Cook: 50mins | Ready in:

Ingredients

- 1 pkg. 8 ounce"crab classic" imitation crab or real will work too!!

- 2 fresh tomatoes, chopped
- handful fresh basil, torn nicely
- 4 cloves garlic, chopped
- 2 Tablespoons of a fresh hot pepper, minced
- 2 cups fresh mushrooms
- 1cup chopped green bell pepper, half sauteed with mushrooms and 1/2 kept fresh
- 3 scallions
- 1/2 cup finely chopped yellow onion
- 4 eggs
- 1/2 cup chicken broth
- 1 tsp., onion powder
- 3/4 cup grated soy mozzarella
- phyllo sheets about 10
- non-stick spray
- 2 Tablespoons melted butter-easier with a pastry brush

Direction

- First line up a baking pan. I used a 10- ish inch square Pyrex dish. One liberal spray with no-stick. Next, layer the filo with a spray on each, 4 -6 layers of filo. Spray again on top of filo. Set aside.
- Set the oven for 350 degrees F.
- Sauté the mushrooms and 1/2 cup green pepper, 5 - 10 mins after the mushrooms lose their liquid. Set aside to cool.
- Collect in a mixing bowl the veggies and wannabe crab. Incorporate sautéed veggies, and arrange filling pieces on the filo crust.
- (I held out the tomatoes and cheese to position on top on the filling. (Soy cheese doesn't melt as well as real cheese often, and tomatoes are super juicy and beautiful too, and they make that fake cheese become gooey!)
- Mix the eggs and broth together, include the onion powder and pour over the filling.
- Top Layer:
- Layer balance of filo sheets in four layers. (Don't worry if a sheet is torn, it gives extra crunch!! use it all and cover the whole top, spraying or using the melted butter on each of the top filo layers which I did.
- Bake about an hour, or until golden and a long toothpick comes out clean. After about 50

minutes, I turned my oven up to 370 and it colored out beautifully, and the eggs were cooked.

88. Easy Quiche Recipe

Serving: 6 | Prep: | Cook: 30mins | Ready in:

Ingredients

- 3/4 cup pastry mix
- 3/4 cup cream
- 3/4 cup milk
- 3 eggs, beaten
- 1 cup grated cheese
- 1 chopped onion
- 100g chopped ham
- salt and pepper

Direction

- Mix all ingredients together. Pour into a greased 10 inch quiche dish and bake at 180deg C for half an hour.
- To make a vegetarian version, substitute 100gms sliced mushrooms for the ham.

89. Easy Swiss Cheesy Bacon Quiche Recipe

Serving: 6 | Prep: | Cook: 40mins | Ready in:

Ingredients

- 12 slices bacon
- 1 cup shredded swiss cheese (4 ounces)
- 1/3 cup onion
- 1/2 cup biscuit mix
- 1 cup whole milk
- 1/8 tsp black pepper
- 2 eggs

Direction

- Preheat oven to 400.
- Fry bacon crisp and let drain on paper towels.
- Meanwhile, finely chop the onion.
- Grease a regular 9 inch pie plate.
- Crumble the bacon into the pie plate. Sprinkle onion over the bacon, then sprinkle the cheese over.
- In a small bowl, beat the eggs, add milk, biscuit mix, and pepper.
- Stir these ingredients together until blended, then pour evenly over contents of the pie plate.
- Bake for 35 to 40 minutes. (Knife inserted near center should come out clean and top should be browned.)
- Let sit 5 minutes, then slice into 6-8 wedges and serve.

90. Easy Turkey Veggie Frittata Recipe

Serving: 0 | Prep: | Cook: 45mins | Ready in:

Ingredients

- 10 Large eggs beaten
- 4 Tbsp olive oil
- 1 Large or 2 small zucchini chopped
- 1 Medium onion finely chopped
- 2 Stalks celery finely chopped
- 2 carrots, peeled and finely chopped
- 1/2 Yellow and 1/2 red bell pepper chopped-any color will work
- Two Medium tomatoes roughly chopped
- 4 Slices deli turkey roughly chopped
- 5 Heaping Tbsp low fat cottage cheese
- 3/4 Cup Shredded cheese (I used Sargento Swiss and gruyere)
- kosher salt
- fresh ground pepper

Direction

- In a large mixing bowl beat eggs and add a big pinch of salt and a few grinds of pepper.

- Add Cottage Cheese and whisk again for 30 seconds.
- Set aside and go to work on your veggies.
- Heat Oil over medium high heat in a 12 inch sauté pan that is safe to place in the oven.
- Chop all the veggies and set aside on a large cutting board.
- Add the onion, celery and carrot to the hot oil and sauté for 2-3 minutes stirring constantly.
- Add bell pepper, tomatoes, zucchini and sliced turkey; sauté for 3-5 more minutes stirring frequently.
- Make sure you season the pan with a bit of salt and pepper after each new set of ingredients is added.
- Pour in the egg mixture, sprinkle the shredded cheese over the top, reduce heat to medium and cook for another 3-5 minutes stirring only occasionally.
- Transfer your sauté pan to the oven at least two rungs from the top and watch it like a hawk from this point forward. It won't take more than 3-5 minutes.
- Once the top begins to brown slightly remove from the oven and let stand for 2-3 minutes. Cut into pie sized slices and serve with a side salad.

91. Egg And Bacon Flan Recipe

Serving: 6 | Prep: | Cook: 1hours | Ready in:

Ingredients

- shortcrust pastry
- Strong cheese - Cheddar is best
- 3 medium onions, sliced
- 6 - 8 rashers smoked back bacon
- 5 eggs
- Half a cup of milk
- black pepper
- An alternative is to add enough flour and a little milk to leftover mashed potatoes to make a dough and use instead of the pastry. It tastes great.

Direction

- Line a 12", shallow, round baking dish with either the pastry or the potato dough.
- Fry the onions in a little oil until tender.
- Roughly chop the bacon, add to the onions and fry until the bacon is just cooked.
- Slice the cheese and cover the bottom of the dish with a generous layer (half an inch or so).
- Cover with the bacon and onions.
- Beat the eggs and milk, add the black pepper (three or four twists of the mill).
- Pour the liquid over the filling and bake in the centre of a moderate oven for about 40 minutes or until the flan is set and nicely brown on the top.
- Delicious hot or cold and freezes well.

92. Egg And Bacon Flan Quiche Recipe

Serving: 6 | Prep: | Cook: 50mins | Ready in:

Ingredients

- Pastry:
- 1 cup   Plain flour
- ¼ tsp   salt
- 80 g   butter
- 2-3 tbls   Cold water
- Filling:
- 1 pack   Lardons (you could use 6 slices of bacon, chopped)
- ½   Large onion, roughly chopped
- 80 g   Strong cheese, grated
- 4   Large eggs
- ¼ tsp   salt
- ¼ tsp   ground black pepper
- ⅛ tsp   cayenne pepper
- 1   Large tomato, thinly sliced

Direction

- Place the flour, salt and butter into a food processer and whizz for 30 seconds or until a ball starts to form. Add the water and whizz again until the pastry leaves the sides - no more than 2 minutes. This can be done by hand.
- Wrap the pastry ball in cling film or foil and place into the fridge for 40 minutes.
- Heat the oven to 425°F/220°C/Gas Mark 7 (Hot)
- Use a floured rolling pin and roll out the pastry so it is about 2 inches larger than a 9 inch quiche pan. Fold into quarters and place it into the dish.
- Unfold and press the party into the bottom and sides. Cut the pastry about 1 inch above the lip of the pan.
- Carefully line the pastry with a sheet of foil and bake for 10 minutes.
- Beat the eggs, salt, cayenne and black pepper together in a medium bowl.
- Cook the lardons. They don't have to be crisp unless you like them that way. Just cooked will do.
- Remove foil carefully and bake for another 2 minutes.
- Take the pastry case from the oven and turn the heat down to 325°F/150°C/Gas Mark 3 (Low)
- Sprinkle the lardons, most of the grated cheese (leave half a handful) and the onions over the base of the pie crust. Pour in the egg mix and sprinkle the remaining cheese on top. Place the tomato slices on the top of the cheese - leave spaces if you like crispy bits of cheese.
- Bake for 45-50 minutes or until a knife comes out clean.

93. Elaines Quiche In A Cakepan Recipe

Serving: 4 | Prep: | Cook: 45mins | Ready in:

Ingredients

- bacon, enough to completely line the pan, approx 11 - 12 slices
- 9 whole eggs
- onion or shallot greens (amount to your preference)
- 1/4 tsp fried rosemary (or 1 tsp fresh)
- salt & pepper to taste

Direction

- Arrange the bacon as illustrated.
- Bake at 350*F until crisp.
- Remove from oven, and drain off the excess fat.
- Lower oven temp to 325*F.
- Combine the eggs, rosemary, onion greens and salt/pepper.
- Mix well.
- Pour mixture into the pan, and bake until set.
- Served hot or cold, this is your preference!
- Variation:
- Add some grated Old, Mozzarella, or Swiss cheese, or all three.

94. Elegant Quiche Recipe

Serving: 8 | Prep: | Cook: 60mins | Ready in:

Ingredients

- 10" spring form pan (good quality)
- 1 tsp dry mustard
- 1 crust to overlap the pan
- 4-5 cups shredded sharp cheddar (easier to shred if place in freezer for 30 minutes) or any cheese you like
- 6 eggs
- 1 qt +1/2 pint heavy cream
- 1-2 cups shredded raw spinach (mainly for color
- sea salt and fresh ground pepper

Direction

- Preheat the oven to 450 degrees.

- Place the rolled dough into the spring form pan and let dough hang over the sides.
- Sprinkle with the dry mustard.
- Place 1/2 of the cheese in the pan.
- Layer the Spinach on top of the cheese.
- Sprinkle with salt and pepper.
- Add remaining cheese.
- Whisk the eggs and cream together and pour slowly into the pan.
- Make sure all of the ingredients are covered with the liquid.
- Take a rolling pin or jar and roll around the top edge of the pan to remove the excess crust.
- Place in the oven on a sheet pan and turn the oven down to 325 degrees.
- Bake until the center is somewhat jiggly (it will continue to settle as it cools down) about 60-70 minutes.
- After allowing to cool slightly (15 - 20 Minutes) remove the sides of the pan.
- Use a very sharp knife to cut into wedges.
- If you feel the quiche is browning too quickly cover with aluminum foil.

95. Estelles Quiche Recipe

Serving: 6 | Prep: | Cook: 45mins | Ready in:

Ingredients

- 1 (9 inch) UNBAKED pie shell
- 1 small onion
- 1 T. butter
- 8 slices cooked bacon, crumbled
- 1 c. grated cheese (Swiss or Chedder)
- 1/2 c. chopped spinach, drained well
- 5 to 6 eggs
- 1 1/2 c. milk or heavy cream
- 1/2 t. salt
- 1/8 t. pepper

Direction

- Sauté onion with butter until onion is translucent.

- Sprinkle bacon, cheese, and onion into bottom of unbaked pie shell.
- Mix eggs in bowl; add milk, spinach, salt, and pepper. Mix well.
- Pour egg mixture over bacon mix in pie shell.
- Bake at 350 degrees for 45 to 50 minutes.
- Cool 10 minutes and serve.

96. Even Easier Then Quiche Recipe

Serving: 6 | Prep: | Cook: 35mins | Ready in:

Ingredients

- 1 box garlic and cheese croutons
- 2 cups shredded cheddar cheese
- 1/2- 1 cup of whatever quiche flavoring you like(veggies, bacon, etc)
- 2 cups milk
- 4 eggs

Direction

- Layer croutons, cheese and flavorings in well-buttered 9/13 baking dish.
- Mix eggs and milk well (I blend in blender).
- Pour over filling.
- THIS IS THE ONLY IMPORTANT PART:
- Let it sit covered for at least an hour in fridge because croutons need time to soak up egg mixture.
- Overnight is fine too.
- Bake uncovered at 350 for at least 35 minutes or until top is golden brown.

97. Everything Crustless Quiche Recipe

Serving: 6 | Prep: | Cook: 30mins | Ready in:

Ingredients

- 6 eggs
- 3 cups cheese
- 1/2 yellow onion
- 1/2 red onion
- 10 mushrooms cleaned and sliced
- 1/4 yellow bell pepper sliced thinly
- 1 bunch fresh spinach boiled and drained
- salt & pepper to taste

Direction

- Preheat oven to 350 degrees
- 1. Sauté the onions, mushrooms, bell pepper. Beat the eggs in a bowl and add the rest of the ingredients and mix together well and then place in a quiche dish sprayed with baking spray and put in the oven for about 30 minutes.

98. Fab Sausage Quiche Recipe

Serving: 8 | Prep: | Cook: 60mins | Ready in:

Ingredients

- Pillsbury ready to go pie crust (DIVA's don't make their own! wink, wink)
- 6 eggs - I use the free range brown vegetarian fed (what else?)
- 2 cups Half & Half
- 2 cups grated swiss cheese
- 2 cups American grated (I use the block Land O' Lakes, but any fave block American will do).
- Jimmy Dean sausage (in your fave flavor-I use regular) in the tube
- 1 tsp salt
- 1 tsp pepper

Direction

- Place pie crust in deep dish pie dish and bake at 425 for 6 minutes
- Brown the Jimmy Dean sausage, drain excess fat and set aside.

- Beat eggs and Half & Half together, add 1 tsp. salt and 1 tsp. pepper
- Place 1 cup of Swiss and 1 cup of American in pie dish.
- Place browned JD sausage on top of that.
- Place 1 c. Swiss and 1 c. American cheese on top of sausage.
- Pour egg mixture over top and Bake at 425 for 15 minutes and then turn down to 350 for another 30-45 min. At 30 minutes check to see if it is done, you can tell be browned top and firmness!
- Enjoy your DIVA breakfast!! Let me know how you LOVE it!!

99. Fabulous Quiche Lorraine Recipe

Serving: 8 | Prep: | Cook: 40mins | Ready in:

Ingredients

- 1 single pastry shell
- 3/4b bacon (uncooked)
- 1/2 lb swiss cheese (grated)
- 4 eggs
- 1 tsp. flour
- 1/2 tsp. salt
- 1/8 - 1/4 tsp. cayenne pepper
- 1/8 - 1/4 tsp. nutmeg
- 2 cups milk
- 1 tsp. melted butter
- Optional:
- chopped onions
- green chiles on the bottom layer (full chili)
- Chopped chiles throughout mixture
- No bacon for Vegetarians

Direction

- Line a 9" pan (quiche pan if available) with pastry.
- Fry bacon until crisp (you will be breaking it up later).

- Grate cheese, and then mix cheese and broken up fried bacon in a bowl.
- Beat eggs in a bowl. Add flour, salt, cayenne and nutmeg, mix lightly.
- Add milk, melted butter, mix lightly.
- Layer the grated cheese and bacon into the pastry.
- Pour the mixture (it is referred to as custard) over the cheese and bacon.
- Bake at 375 degrees for 40-45 minutes until set. It should get a little brown here and there on the top.
- Allow to rest for about 15 minutes or until you can't stand it anymore, cut into wedges (if sharing) or grab a fork and eat until you can't get another bite in. OH MAN, this is good stuff.
- A great recipe that can be heated up later in the microwave. OH Man, this is good stuff.
- I peeled the top off in the last couple of pics to show how juicy the quiche is and these were pics of the quiche microwaved about a minute the next day. The slice should be cut into three pieces and spread out evenly around the plate for even heating.

100. Festive Italian Quiche Recipe

Serving: 0 | Prep: | Cook: 1hours | Ready in:

Ingredients

- 1 unbaked 9-inch pie shell
- 2 Tbsp. oil
- 2 cups of chopped zucchini
- 1/2 cup of chopped onion
- 1 garlic clove, minced
- 1 1/4 cups shredded mozzarella cheese
- 3 eggs beaten
- 1 cup cottage or ricotta cheese
- 1/3 cup of milk
- 1/2 tsp. salt
- Freshly ground pepper

- tomato sauce, recipe follows,
- (Dried) Parsley, (Dried) Oregano, Fresh garlic, Dried Basil, salt & Pepper

Direction

- Preheat oven to 350 degrees. Bake pie shell 10 minutes. Remove from oven and let cool. Increase oven temperature to 375 degrees. Heat oil in medium skillet over medium-high heat. Add zucchini, onion and garlic and sauté until tender, about 10 minutes. Spread evenly in pie shell.
- Mix 1 cup mozzarella with remaining ingredients except sauce. Spoon over vegetables and sprinkle with remaining cheese. Bake until knife inserted near center comes out clean, about 40 minutes. Let stand 5 minutes, then cut into wedges and serve with Tomato Sauce.
- Tomato Sauce:
- 1 15-ounce can tomato sauce
- 1 Tbsp. dried parsley flakes
- 1 tsp. dried oregano
- 1/2 tsp. dried basil leaves, crumbled
- 1 clove of garlic, or more, minced
- Salt and freshly ground pepper
- Simmer ingredients in medium saucepan for 15 minutes, stirring occasionally.

101. Flourless Quiche Recipe

Serving: 4 | Prep: | Cook: 40mins | Ready in:

Ingredients

- 4 eggs
- 1/2 cup onion, finely chopped
- 1/2 cup cooked meat (chicken, beef, lean pork, etc) finely chopped
- 1/2 cup milk
- 4 ounces grated cheese
- 2 tablespoons milk powder (optional; adds body and additional protein)
- salt, pepper, freshly-ground nutmeg (to taste)

- 1 tablespoon olive oil
- non-stick cooking spray

Direction

- Sauté onion in olive oil, until tender and translucent. Allow to cool.
- In large bowl, beat eggs.
- Add remaining ingredients to bowl; stir to combine.
- Spray gratin pan, shallow pie pan, or other cooking pan with non-stick spray. Pour mixture into pan.
- Place the quiche pan into a larger baking pan (such as a lasagna pan). Add about 1/2 inch to 3/4 inch of hot water to the larger pan. Avoid getting water into quiche mixture!
- Bake at 300 degrees until quiche is firm, but still jiggles when shaken, about 40 minutes.

---

102. Fluffy Asparagus Quiche Recipe

Serving: 8 | Prep: | Cook: 60mins | Ready in:

Ingredients

- 1 deep-dish pie crust, cooked according to packaged directions
- 8-10 stalks of fresh asparagus, trimmed and cut into bite size pieces
- 5 large eggs
- 1/4 cup heavy cream
- 1 teaspoon Dijon mustard
- 1/2 teaspoon salt
- 1/4 teaspoon cayenne pepper
- 1/4 teaspoon paprika
- 1 cup cottage cheese (I used small curd)
- 3/4 lb. swiss cheese (I used a .8 lb block of Jarlsberg semi-soft swiss)
- 4 pieces bacon, cooked and crumbled

Direction

- Preheat oven to 350 degrees.

- Boil half a cup of water is small saucepan and add asparagus pieces. Cover and turn off the heat. Let the asparagus steam while you are preparing the rest of the dish.
- In a large bowl, beat the eggs with an electric beater until well blended. Blend in the cream, mustard, salt, pepper and paprika. With a spoon, stir in cheese. Combine thoroughly.
- Drain asparagus. Lay out asparagus pieces flat in the bottom of the cooked pie crust.
- Pour egg mixture over the asparagus. Place pie into preheated oven.
- Bake for 40-45 minutes, or until knife inserted in the middle comes out clean.
- Remove from oven and sprinkle crumbled bacon over top of cooked quiche.
- Allow to cool for 5-10 minutes before slicing and serving.

---

103. Four Cheese And Crab Quiche Recipe

Serving: 8 | Prep: | Cook: 45mins | Ready in:

Ingredients

- 1/2 cup boiling water
- 1/2 cup vegetable oil
- 2 cups flour
- 1 pinch salt
- 1/2 cup shredded swiss cheese
- 1/2 cup shredded sharp cheddar cheese
- 1/2 cup crumbled feta cheese
- 1/2 cup grated romano cheese
- 4 eggs
- 1 pint heavy cream
- 1/2 cup cubed zucchini
- 1 cup shredded crab meat
- 1/4 teaspoon salt
- 1 teaspoon freshly-ground black pepper
- 1/4 teaspoon cayenne pepper
- 1/4 teaspoon nutmeg

Direction

- Combine water, oil, flour and salt then mix with fork and press into large quiche pan.
- Combine eggs, cream and seasonings then whisk for 1 minute.
- Put cheeses, vegetable and crab into prepared shell.
- Pour liquid over filling and bake at 425 for 15 minutes then reduce to 350 and bake 45 minutes.

104.   Freakin Awesome Quiche Recipe

Serving: 10 | Prep: | Cook: 40mins | Ready in:

Ingredients

- 3 regular pie shells or 2 deep-dish pie shells (I get the frozen pre-made ones)
- 1 container of egg Beaters All Whites
- 1 cup skim milk
- 1 package chopped frozen spinach
- 1 package of diced up ham from the deli section (I used 96% fat free)
- 1 red bell pepper
- 1 onion
- 10 cherry tomatoes, or 5-6 roma tomatoes (or a combination of both)
- a teaspoon olive oil
- salt, to taste.
- 1 package sliced up mushrooms
- 4 slices American cheese
- Mozzerella cheese (yes you can use string cheese!)
- Low-fat shredded cheddar cheese

Direction

- Preheat oven to 340.
- Stick the bottoms of the pie crusts with a fork a few times. Then put them into the oven and cook them for 8-10 minutes. Meanwhile…
- Chop onion, red bell pepper, and tomatoes into small pieces. Sauté in skillet with olive oil until tender. Remove from skillet when done.

- Put mushrooms in skillet and cook till done.
- Defrost frozen spinach. Squeeze excess water out of spinach.
- Dump container of egg whites into a big, big bowl. Add milk. Stir.
- Add the sautéed onion, pepper, and tomato. Add spinach. Add mushrooms. Stir again.
- Add a little salt, to taste (I use a sea salt grinder and grind about 5 times).
- Dump in ham and stir together.
- Tear apart American cheese slices and add to the mixture.
- Add mozzarella or cut up mozzarella cheese stick and add to mixture.
- When all the ingredients are mixed up, use a deep spoon and spoon the mixture into the pie shells.
- Bake for 35 minutes at 340 degrees.
- Remove from oven, sprinkle shredded cheddar cheese on top. Replace quiches in oven and cook another 5-10 minutes.

105.   Fresh Basil And Tomato Quiche With 3 Cheeses Recipe

Serving: 6 | Prep: | Cook: 40mins | Ready in:

Ingredients

- 1 cup Shredded cheddar cheese
- 1 cup Shredded monterey jack cheese
- 1 cup Shredded swiss cheese
- 1 tablespoon All purpose flour
- 6 eggs, beaten
- 1/2 cup Half & Half
- 3 roma tomatoes, sliced in circles
- 1/2 cup Fresh Chopped basil leaves

Direction

- Preheat oven to 350 degrees.
- Coat an 8 inch quiche dish with non-stick spray.
- Combine cheeses.

- In a small bowl toss 1 cup of combined cheeses with flour.
- Place the cheese/flour mixture in bottom of quiche pan.
- Add the rest of the cheese on top.
- Lightly whisk eggs together, add half & half and whisk till frothy.
- Pour egg mixture over cheeses.
- Sprinkle shredded basil leaves on top of egg mixture and lay tomato slices on top.
- Bake 35-40 minutes until center is nicely browned and domed.
- Let sit out for at least 20 minutes so eggs will set.

106.   Garden Vegetable Quiche Recipe

Serving: 6 | Prep: | Cook: 40mins | Ready in:

Ingredients

- 1 (9 or 10 inch) pie crust
- 1 cup onion, chopped
- 1 green bell pepper, chopped
- 1 cup fresh broccoli, chopped
- 1 cup fresh tomatoes, seeded and diced
- 1/2 cup fresh mushrooms, sliced
- 2 tablespoons butter
- 1 teaspoon garlic, minced
- salt to taste
- 1/2 teaspoon ground black pepper
- 1/2 cup mozzarella cheese, shredded
- 1/4 cup parmesan cheese, grated
- 5 eggs
- 1/4 cup milk

Direction

- Line a 9 or 10 inch pie pan with pie crust.
- Line crust with a double thickness of aluminum foil.
- Bake at 450 degrees for 5 minutes. Remove foil and bake an additional 5 minutes.

- Place on rack and let cool while preparing remaining ingredients.
- In large skillet, melt butter. Add onion, green bell pepper, broccoli, tomatoes and mushrooms. Sauté until vegetables are softened.
- Add garlic, salt and pepper. Mix well. Remove from heat.
- Spoon vegetables into crust.
- Sprinkle with cheeses.
- Whisk together eggs and milk. Pour over vegetables.
- Bake at 350 degrees for 30 to 40 minutes or until knife inserted near center comes out clean.
- If edges get too brown, cover edges with foil during baking.
- Let stand 5 minutes before slicing.

107.   Garlic And Sweet Potato Quiche Recipe

Serving: 6 | Prep: | Cook: 60mins | Ready in:

Ingredients

- 30g unsalted butter, melted
- 375g puff pastry
- 1/2 butternut squash, peeled and cut into 2cm wedges
- 3 tbsp olive oil
- 2 heads garlic, cloves peeled
- 1 tbsp balsamic vinegar
- 1 1/2 tbsp caster sugar
- 1 tsp chopped rosemary
- 1 tsp chopped thyme
- 130g goats cheese
- 2 eggs
- 100ml double cream
- 100ml creme fraiche

Direction

- Preheat the oven to 180C/gas mark 4.

- Brush a 22cm tin with butter, roll out pastry and line the tin. Brush it with more butter and bake for 30 mins (or until cooked).
- Spread the squash over an oven tray, sprinkle with a little oil and salt, and roast for 30 mins.
- Meanwhile, boil the garlic in a small pan for 3 mins, then drain.
- Fry the garlic in a couple of tablespoons of oil for a couple of minutes, then add vinegar and 100ml water, and simmer for 10 mins.
- Add the sugar, herbs and 1/2 tsp. salt and simmer for 10 more mins to make a caramel syrup.
- Whisk together eggs, creams, 1/2 tsp. salt and some black pepper.
- Put the squash in the pastry case, scatter with garlic (& syrup) and goat's cheese, and then pour over the eggy cream.
- Turn the oven to 170C/gas mark 3 and bake for 35-45 minutes, until the top is golden brown.

108.   Ham With Cheese And Broccoli Quiche Recipe

Serving: 6 | Prep: | Cook: 50mins | Ready in:

Ingredients

- 1 refrigerated pie crust
- 1 cup milk (not skim or 1%)
- 4 - 6 eggs, slightly beaten (depending on the size)
- 1/4 tsp. dry mustard
- 1/8 tsp. pepper
- a dash of Tobasco or other hot sauce (just a dash)
- 1 cup cooked ham, cubed
- 1-1/2 cups cheddar cheese, shredded (I like Tex Mex shredded)
- 1 cup frozen broccoli flowerets, thawed
- Note: I have also used frozen, thawed and well drained spinach.
- 1/2 onion, finely chopped

Direction

- Prepare pie crust according to package directions for "filled one-crust pie"
- Heat oven to 350 degrees F.
- In medium bowl, combine milk, eggs, dry mustard, pepper and Tabasco sauce.
- Set aside.
- Layer ham, cheese, broccoli and onion in pie crust.
- Pour egg mixture over ham, cheese and broccoli.
- Bake for 40 to 50 minutes or until knife inserted in center comes out clean.
- Cool 5-10 minutes before serving.

109.   Ham And Green Chile Bite Size Quiche Recipe

Serving: 42 | Prep: | Cook: 20mins | Ready in:

Ingredients

- 3/4 - 1 cup finely diced ham
- 3-4 tablespoons chopped canned green chiles
- 1/4 cup minced green onion
- 1 2/3 cups shredded monterey jack cheese
- 1 15-oz. package prepared pie crusts (2 crusts)
- 5 eggs
- 1 2/3 cups sour cream

Direction

- Heat oven to 375 degrees F. On a lightly floured board, roll out the pie crust. Using a 3-inch cutter, cut out 42 circles; re-roll scraps as needed. Fit circles into bottoms and slightly up sides of lightly greased 2 1/2-inch muffin pans.
- Meanwhile, in a medium bowl, mix together ham, chiles, onion and cheese and divide equally among muffin cups. In large bowl, beat together eggs, add sour cream and stir until smooth. Spoon about 1 tablespoon into each muffin cup.

- Bake until puffed and light brown, 20-25 minutes. Cool in pans 5 minutes; lift out. Serve warm or let cool on wire racks.
- If made ahead, wrap cooled quiches airtight, and refrigerate overnight. Reheat, uncovered, in a 350 degrees F. oven for about 10 minutes.
- Makes 3 1/2 dozen.
- Also try serving alongside Bacon and Mushroom Bite Size Quiche.

110. Ham 'n' Cheese Quiche

Serving: 6 | Prep: | Cook: 45mins | Ready in:

Ingredients

- 1 package (14.1 ounces) refrigerated pie crust
- 2 cups diced fully cooked ham
- 2 cups shredded sharp cheddar cheese
- 2 teaspoons dried minced onion
- 4 large eggs
- 2 cups half-and-half cream
- 1/2 teaspoon salt
- 1/4 teaspoon pepper

Direction

- Preheat oven to 400°. Unroll pie crusts into two 9-in. pie plates; flute edges. Line unpricked pie crusts with a double thickness of heavy-duty foil. Fill with pie weights, dried beans or uncooked rice. Bake until light golden brown, 10-12 minutes. Remove foil and weights; bake until bottom is golden brown, 3-5 minutes longer or Cool on wire racks.
- Divide ham, cheese and onion between shells. In a large bowl, whisk eggs, cream, salt and pepper until blended. Pour into crusts. Cover edges loosely with foil. Bake until a knife inserted in the center comes out clean, 35-40 minutes. Let stand 5-10 minutes before cutting.
- Freeze option: Cover and freeze unbaked quiche. To use, remove from freezer 30 minutes before baking (do not thaw). Preheat oven to 350°. Place quiche on a baking sheet;

cover edge loosely with foil. Bake as directed, increasing time as necessary for a knife inserted in the center to come out clean.
- Note: Let pie weights cool before storing. Beans and rice may be reused for pie weights, but not for cooking.
- Nutrition Facts
- 1 piece: 349 calories, 23g fat (12g saturated fat), 132mg cholesterol, 596mg sodium, 20g carbohydrate (3g sugars, 0 fiber), 13g protein.

111. Hash Brown Quiche Recipe

Serving: 8 | Prep: | Cook: 25mins | Ready in:

Ingredients

- 3 cups shredded hash brown potatoes
- 1/3 cup butter, melted
- seasoning salt to taste
- 1 cup diced cooked ham
- 1/4 cup chopped onion
- 1 cup shredded cheddar cheese
- 2 eggs
- 1/2 cup milk
- salt and pepper to taste

Direction

- Preheat oven to 425 degrees F (220 degrees C).
- Press hash browns onto the bottom and sides of a 9 inch pie dish.
- Drizzle with melted butter, and sprinkle with seasoning salt.
- Bake in preheated oven for 20 minutes, or until beginning to brown.
- In a small bowl, combine ham, onion and shredded cheese.
- In a separate bowl, whisk together eggs, milk, salt, pepper, and a little seasoning salt.
- When crust is ready, spread ham mixture on the bottom, and then cover with egg mixture.
- Reduce oven temperature to 350 degrees F (175 degrees C.)

- Bake in preheated oven for 20 to 25 minutes, or until filling is puffed and golden brown.
- ~
- FOOTNOTE:
- You can bake this quiche, and refrigerate for up to 2 days in advance, then reheat in the microwave. It also freezes well.

112. Hashbrown Quiche With Mushrooms Recipe

Serving: 8 | Prep: | Cook: 42mins | Ready in:

Ingredients

- 20 oz. package ORE IDA pepper and Onion Hashbrown potatoes
- 1/4 cup margarine, melted (original recipe calls for 1/2 cup but 1/4 is fine)
- 1 package fresh mushrooms, sliced (about 1 1/2 cups)
- 2 cups shredded cheese (try monterey jack, colby, or mild cheddar)
- 4 green onions with tops, chopped
- 2 eggs, beaten (I use 1/2 cup egg substitute)
- 1/2 cup milk

Direction

- Spray 10 inch square baking dish (or similar size dish) with non-stick spray.
- Melt margarine and pour into dish.
- Press hashbrowns into dish with margarine and bake at 425 for 25 minutes.
- Remove from oven and put 1 cup of shredded cheese on this, then onions and mushrooms, then last cup of cheese.
- Mix eggs and milk and pour over the top.
- Bake for another 20-25 minutes at 425.

113. ITALIAN ZUCCHINI QUICHE Recipe

Serving: 6 | Prep: | Cook: 20mins | Ready in:

Ingredients

- 4 cups thinly sliced zucchini
- 1 cup chopped onion
- ¼ to ½ cup margarine
- ½ cup chopped parsley or 2 T. dried flakes
- ½ t. salt
- ½ t. pepper
- ¼ t. garlic powder
- ¼ t. basil
- ¼ t. oregano leaves
- 2 beaten eggs
- 8 oz. (2 cups) shredded mozzarella or natural muenster cheese.
- 2 t. prepared mustard (optional)

Direction

- Sauté zucchini and onion in margarine for 10 min.
- Stir in seasonings.
- Combine eggs and cheese; stir into vegetables.
- Spread unbaked pie crust with mustard, if desired.
- Pour vegetable mixture into crust.
- Bake @ 375 deg. for 18 to 20 minutes or until center is set.

114. Impossible Quiche Recipe

Serving: 6 | Prep: | Cook: 40mins | Ready in:

Ingredients

- 2 cups ham, cubed
- 1 cup shredded swiss cheese
- 1/2 cup onion
- 4 eggs
- 2 cups milk

- 1 cup Bisquick
- 1/4 tsp salt
- 1/8 tsp pepper

Direction

- Sauté onions until soft.
- Sprinkle ham, cheese and onions in a pie plate.
- Beat remaining ingredients until smooth.
- Pour into pie plate over the ham, cheese and onions.
- Bake at 400 degrees for 35 to 40 minutes.

115. Italian Sausage & Potato Tart Recipe

Serving: 8 | Prep: | Cook: 20mins | Ready in:

Ingredients

- 1 batch of pastry already made
- 6 eggs beaten
- 3-4 sweet Italian sausages opened and cooked
- Sage
- parsley
- 1 cup cheese
- 1/4 cup sherry
- 1 can sliced potatoes drained

Direction

- 1. Tart pan with removable bottom sprayed with non-stick and then place the pastry in it and stab with fork and bake blind in a 350 degree preheated oven for about 10-15 minutes.
- 2. Remove the tart shell from the oven and place in the seasoned cooked sausage and top with the beaten eggs.
- 3. Top with the sliced potatoes and sprinkle with cheese and then bake for about 30 minutes in 350 degree oven.

116. Jack O Lantern Quiche Recipe

Serving: 6 | Prep: | Cook: 30mins | Ready in:

Ingredients

- 1 baked pie shell (8")
- 5 slices thick-cut lean bacon
- 12 oz pumpkin, sliced thin
- 2 T thyme, minced
- 3 eggs
- 1-1/2 C cream
- 3/4 tsp salt
- 1/2 tsp hot sauce
- 3 0z fresh mozzarella, shredded
- 3 oz sharp cheddar, shredded

Direction

- Cook the bacon in a heavy skillet until crisp.
- Drain on paper towels.
- Pour out and discard all but one tablespoon of the bacon fat.
- Sauté the pumpkin slices in the remaining bacon fat on medium heat until just starting to soften, about 5 minutes.
- Remove from heat and toss the pumpkin slices with 2/3 of the thyme.
- In a bowl, beat the eggs briefly and then add the cream, salt and hot sauce, mixing well.
- Lay the pumpkin slices in the pie shell.
- Chop and add the bacon, then the cheeses, reserving 2 tablespoons of cheddar.
- Pour in the egg mixture.
- Scatter the remaining cheese and thyme over the quiche and bake about 30 minutes in a preheated 375° oven until a tester comes out clean.
- If adding decorations to the quiche, cook them until just tender beforehand and place them on the surface after the quiche has baked about 20 minutes and the custard has started to set up.

117. Jalapeño Popper Quiche Recipe

Serving: 8 | Prep: | Cook: | Ready in:

Ingredients

- Jalapeño Popper Quiche Added by Katie Metz de Martínez
- at http://www.hispanickitchen.com
- This quiche is like a jalapeno popper for breakfast! Yum!
- Quiche INGREDIENTS:
- * 9" pie crust
- * 1/2 cup cream cheese
- * 2 jalapenos, diced, and 1 sliced into 6 rounds
- * 1/2 cup cream
- * 1/2 cup half-and-half
- * 4 large eggs (or 5 small)
- * 1/8 teaspoon nutmeg
- * 1/8 teaspoon paprika
- * 1/8 teaspoon salt
- * 1/2 cup grated cheddar-jack

Direction

- Beat the eggs together in a bowl
- Add the hot cream mixture to the eggs and combine well
- Add all the spices and salt
- Pour into the crust and bake for 30 minutes
- After 30 minutes, arrange the jalapeno slices over the top in a circle and return to oven for 10 minutes
- Sprinkle with cheese and bake another 5 minutes
- Cool 30-45 minutes before serving or cool completely and serve it cold.

118. Jetts Broccoli Cheese Quiche Recipe

Serving: 6 | Prep: | Cook: 40mins | Ready in:

Ingredients

- 1 Cup chopped broccoli
- 1 Cup chopped onions
- 1 cup chopped fresh mushrooms
- 5 eggs
- 1/3 Cup milk
- 1/3 Cup mayonnaise
- 1 Cup shredded sharp cheddar cheese
- 1 Frozen deep-dish pie crust (9 inch)

Direction

- Heat oven to 350 degrees F.
- Cook vegetables in skillet sprayed with cooking spray on medium heat 5 minutes, or until tender. Remove from heat.
- Beat eggs, mayonnaise and milk in medium bowl with whisk until well blended. Stir in vegetable mixture and cheese. Pour into pie crust.
- Place on baking sheet.
- Bake 40-45 minutes or until center of quiche is set and top is golden brown. Let stand 10 minutes before slicing.
- ~Love never fails
- *For this quiche, I grated some fresh carrots and added to the mix - loved the texture

119. Jetts Spinach Cheese Quiche Recipe

Serving: 8 | Prep: | Cook: 45mins | Ready in:

Ingredients

- 1 large bag frozen spinach leaves (thawed & drained)
- 1 small zuchinni (grated)
- 1 cup grated carrots
- 1 cup chopped onion
- 5 eggs
- 1/3 Cup mayonnaise
- 1/3 Cup milk
- 1/2 Cup shredded cheddar cheese

- 1/2 Cup shredded mozzarella cheese
- 3 Tablespoons olive oil
- 1 large unbaked deep dish pie shell

Direction

- Preheat oven to 375 degrees F.
- In a medium size bowl add eggs, mayonnaise, milk - mix well and set aside.
- In a large pan add all the vegetables with the olive oil and stir constantly over medium heat for about 5 minutes.
- Add the vegetables to the egg mixture and blend well.
- Place unbaked quiche on a large pan in the middle of the oven.
- Bake for approximately 45 minutes or until quiche is set.
- ~Nothing succeeds like the appearance of success.

120. Joes Best Quiche Lorraine Recipe

Serving: 6 | Prep: | Cook: 40mins | Ready in:

Ingredients

- 1 nine inch frozen pie crust
- 1/2 pound bacon
- 2 cups shredded swiss cheese (I like Jarlsberg)
- 1 3oz. can sliced mushrooms
- 2 cups milk
- 4 large eggs
- 1/4 tsp. nutmeg
- 1 tsp. salt
- 1/4 tsp pepper

Direction

- Fry bacon until grease is rendered, then crumble when cooled.
- Put bacon and shredded cheese into the pie crust, add mushrooms.

- Beat eggs and milk together along with the salt, pepper, and nutmeg.
- Pour the custard into the crust over the cheese, bacon and mushrooms.
- Bake at 375 degrees for 40 mins with a baking pan on rack beneath it to catch any spillage.
- Serve immediately for best results, but I also like it as a leftover if there is any leftover.

121. Junos Summer Quiche Recipe

Serving: 6 | Prep: | Cook: 45mins | Ready in:

Ingredients

- 2 tablespoons olive oil
- 1 medium onion, thiny sliced
- 2 garlic cloves, crushed
- 2 cups fresh spinach, coarsely chopped
- 1/2 cup julienned red bell pepper strips
- 1/3 cup oil-packed sun-dried tomatoes, chopped
- 1 9-inch Wholemeal Crust (recipe included here)
- 2 cups grated cheese - choose from gruyere, Jarlsberg, Swiss, Monterey Jack, Cheddar (Cait says gruyere is the best)
- 2 to 3 eggs
- 1 1/2 cups low-fat milk (or milk substitute)
- 1 medium tomato, thinly sliced
- fresh rosemary sprigs, for garnish
- white pepper
- AND, a combination of any of these:
- 3 tablespoons grated Parmesan or romano cheese
- 1 tablespoon whole wheat flour
- 2 dashes of sea salt
- For the WholeMeal Crust:
- 1/2 cup whole wheat or graham flour
- 1/2 cup unbleached white flour
- dash of sea salt
- 1/3 cup chilled butter, cut into small pieces
- 2 to 3 tablespoons ice water

Direction

- To make the crust:
- Combine the flours and salt in a bowl.
- Using a pastry cutter, or two knives, mix in the chilled butter.
- Continue to blend, rubbing the dough with your fingers if necessary, until the mixture resembles coarse meal.
- Add 2 to 3 tablespoons ice water and mix with your hands until the dough forms a ball.
- Dust your surface with flour and roll out the dough until it is a flat circle 1 inch larger than your pie plate.
- Place it in the plate, pinching the edges decoratively if you wish.
- To make the quiche filling:
- Preheat the oven to 375-degrees F.
- In a saucepan, heat the oil over medium high heat.
- Add the onion and garlic, stirring frequently until they are barely tender.
- Add the spinach, pepper strips and sundried tomatoes.
- Continue cooking for several minutes.
- Spread vegetables evenly over the unbaked bottom crust in a 9-inch pie plate. (You could even use Polenta as a crust for this quiche!)
- Sprinkle over the vegetables the grated cheese of your choice along with the grated Parmesan or Romano, flour and one dash sea salt.
- Whisk together in a bowl the eggs, milk and a dash of sea salt until smooth.
- Pour the custard over the vegetables and cheeses in the crust.
- Place tomato slices decoratively on top of the quiche, along with several fresh sprigs of rosemary.
- Grate some white pepper over it all, in honor of Juno's notoriously peppery temper.
- Bake for 40 to 45 minutes, until puffy, fragrant and golden brown.
- Enjoy!

122.   Kudzoo Quiche From Zoo Atlanta Cookbook Recipe

Serving: 6 | Prep: | Cook: 45mins | Ready in:

Ingredients

- 1 cup heavy cream
- 3 eggs beaten
- 1 cup young, tender kudzu leaves & stems, chopped
- 1/2 teaspoon salt
- pepper to taste
- 1 cup mozarrella cheese
- 9-inch unbaked pastry shell(*Refer to Mama's pie crust recipe, or buy one if preferred)

Direction

- Preheat oven to 350 degrees F.
- Mix all ingredients and turn into pie shell.
- Bake for 35-45 minutes, or until set.
- Serves 4 - 6

123.   Laing Recipe

Serving: 8 | Prep: | Cook: 1hours10mins | Ready in:

Ingredients

- 1 pack (3.5 oz or 100g) dried taro leaves
- 6 cups (3 cans) coconut milk
- 2 cups (1 can) coconut cream
- ½ cup shrimp paste (bagoong or balaw)
- ½ lb. pork shoulder, thinly sliced
- 5 to 7 pieces red chilies
- 1 medium yellow onion, sliced
- ½ cup sliced ginger
- 8 cloves garlic, crushed

Direction

- Combine the coconut milk, pork, ginger, shrimp paste, ginger, onion, and garlic in a cooking pot. Heat the pot and let it boil.

- Once the mixture starts to boil, gently stir to mix the ingredients. Cover the pot and simmer for 15 to 20 minutes. Make sure to stir once in a while to prevent the ingredients from sticking at the bottom of the cooking pot.
- Add the dried taro leaves. Do not stir. Let it stay until the leaves absorb the coconut milk. This takes about 20 to 30 minutes. You can gently push the leaves down so that it can absorb more coconut milk.
- Once the leaves absorb the coconut milk, stir the leaves and then continue to cook for to 10 minutes.
- Pour the coconut cream in the cooking pot. Add the red chilies. Stir. Cook for 10 to 12 minutes more.
- Transfer to a serving plate. Serve.
- Share and enjoy!

124.   Lanas Quick And Delicious Quiche Recipe

Serving: 8 | Prep: | Cook: 90mins | Ready in:

Ingredients

- 1 store bought pie crust, or make your own
- 6 eggs
- a splash of milk
- seasoning to preferred taste, this really depends on what else you add:
- white pepper, sea salt, italian seasoning, nutmeg
- ~
- Yummy Stuff
- ham, turkey, bacon, sausage, peppers, mushrooms, onions, zucchini, eggplant, asparagus, tomatoes, even pineapple and Canadian bacon, you get the picture here, it should just over flow! That's why its a deep dish!
- ~
- cheese between 3/4 cup and 1 1/2 cups of your favorite, or a mix of several!

- ~~~~~~~~~~~~~~~~~~~~~~~~~~~~~~~~~~~~ ~~~~~~~~~~~~~~~~~
- This could be turned into a dessert quiche by using fruit as the goodies and cream cheese and another mellow smooth cheese as the cheese. And try adding splenda to the eggs with some cinnamon and nutmeg.... You get the idea! And a sweet homemade pie crust! You go my Lady Lana!!!

Direction

- Press the dough into the deep dish.
- Toss in all of the goodies, meats, veggies, and that sort of thing.
- Mix the eggs and milk together well.
- Pour over goodies.
- Top with cheese.
- Bake in medium over, 350 F, for about an hour to an hour and a half.
- A knife inserted comes out clean.
- Take out of oven.
- Let sit for 20 minutes.
- Serve and enjoy!
- This can be made ahead in an evening so the next morning breakfast in bed is a snap!!!! Some melon, a slice of quiche, breakfast tea with honey, and a rose to top it off! That is heaven!!!

125.   Leahs Quick Quiche Lorraine Recipe

Serving: 6 | Prep: | Cook: 45mins | Ready in:

Ingredients

- I love bacon and ham, and who doesn't love this combined with cheeses...I do not use half-n-half but whole milk...(as if that was going to help with lessoning the calorie count!) lol
- 5 thick slices on bacon diced
- 1 cup of diced (Bodacious) Baked ham that maybe left over in fridge.
- 1 large onion diced

- 4 jumbo eggs or 5 large eggs
- 1-1/2 cups of three cheeses - I use up whatever is left over before it goes into a downward spiral of unidentifiable cheese - This time I chose brie, parmesan freshly grated, fresh mozzarella cut up and crumbled goat cheeses.
- 2-1/2 tablespoons of flour
- 2 tablespoons freshly minced green scallions or chives
- 1/2 teaspoon of nutmeg in addition to
- 3 or 4 shakes of nutmeg
- 1 teaspoon freshly ground pepper
- salt is really not needed due to the bacon and ham
- 1 tablespoon olive oil
- 1 pastry shell uncooked and chilled.
- ***Equipment Needed:
- Large skillet, one working oven at 350 degrees, several bowls, cookie sheet

Direction

- Take eggs out of refrigerator and let come to room temperature.
- In cold skillet, add olive oil and diced bacon and turn heat onto medium.
- With spoon, stir on occasion to let bacon crisp all over, tis better to allow bacon to cook slowly versus too quick and smoke up the house. Less bacon shrinkage too. (Who knew?!?)
- Remove cooked bacon and put in cut up ham and onions into remaining bacon fat. Cook till onions are translucent and starts to become caramelized.
- While ham and onions are cooking, crack eggs and place into one bowl. Whisk eggs till smooth, add milk, salt and pepper and 1/2 teaspoon of nutmeg. Stir till well combined and set aside.
- Grate and cut up your cheeses and place into a second bowl. Stir cheese till combined then add flour, stirring till flour coats the cheese.
- Return to skillet, and with slotted spoon, drain out caramelized onions and cooked ham. Drain on paper towels and add bacon. Let cool for five minutes.

- Mix bacon mixture into cheese mixture and stir till well combined.
- Pour this mixture into unbaked pie shell.
- Place pie shell onto cookie sheet.
- Pour egg mixture into pie shell over the bacon mixture.
- Add a couple of shakes of ground nutmeg to top along with freshly minced scallions on top of unbaked quiche.
- Carefully, place cookie sheet with quiche sitting on top, into the oven and let bake for 45 minutes at 350 degrees.
- Check if done when taking knife and inserting it, the knife comes out clean.
- Let quiche sit for 20 minutes before serving allowing it to finish "setting up", serve with fresh mixed salad greens and or warm and toasty soup for a perfect luncheon.
- PS, I said to heck with the 20 minutes, and sliced me up a piece immediately - thinking about going for naughty seconds.

126.   Let There Be Quiche Recipe

Serving: 8 | Prep: | Cook: 30mins | Ready in:

Ingredients

- 8 farm eggs (if you can)
- 1/4 c milk
- 2-3 cloves garlic crushed
- 1/4 ts salt
- 3/4 ts pepper
- 1/4 c parmesan cheese grated
- 1/4 c green onions (with some greens) chopped
- 1/2 c swiss cheese shredded
- 2 sm zucchini coarsely grated
- 1 c monterey jack cheese grated

Direction

- In large bowl, beat eggs, milk, garlic, salt, pepper and parmesan. Set aside.

- In pre-made 9 inch pie shell (or make your own, but I use Pillsbury Fold and Bake shells), put an even layer of Swiss cheese, followed by green onion, then zucchini. Sprinkle w jack cheese. Pour egg mixture over all.
- Bake uncovered at 350 degrees for 25-30 minutes or until center is set when touched lightly. Place on wire rack to cool. Serve and room temperature or chilled.

127. Lobster Quiche Recipe

Serving: 6 | Prep: | Cook: 45mins | Ready in:

Ingredients

- 1 - 9" pie shell, unbaked
- 2 T. finely chopped green onions
- 2 T. butter
- 1 1/4 c. diced, canned or fresh cooked lobster
- 1 T. fresh dill
- 4 eggs, slightly beaten
- 2 T. dry white wine
- 1/2 tsp. salt
- 1/4 tsp. white pepper
- 1 1/4 c. heavy cream, whipped

Direction

- Prick bottom of pie shell with a fork and line with foil.
- Fill it with beans or rice (for weight to prevent puffing during prebaking).
- Bake in preheated 400 F oven for 8 minutes.
- Remove foil and item used for weight.
- Bake an additional 3 minutes.
- Reduce oven temperature to 375 F.
- Meanwhile, sauté' onions in butter.
- Spread in the partly cooked pie shell.
- Top with lobster and fresh dill.
- Combine the eggs, wine, salt, pepper, and cream.
- Pour into shell on top of lobster.
- Bake for 25 - 30 minutes or until set.

128. Lovely Lower Fat Cheese Spinach Quiche

Serving: 4 | Prep: | Cook: 50mins | Ready in:

Ingredients

- 1 cup sliced mushrooms
- 1 cup chopped onion
- 1 (10 ounce) package frozen chopped spinach, thawed, drained well
- 1/3 cup low fat milk
- 4 eggs
- 1 cup low fat Shredded mozzarella cheese
- 1 (9 inch) frozen prepared pie shell
- 1/4 cup OSCAR MAYER low fat Real bacon bits (optional)
- seasonings (optional)

Direction

- Preheat oven to 375 degrees F.
- Spray nonstick skillet with cooking spray.
- Add mushrooms and onion; cook 5 min. or until tender.
- Stir in spinach; mix well.
- Add seasoning, (if needed)
- Mix milk and eggs until well blended.
- Add spinach mixture and cheese.
- Pour into pie shell; sprinkle with bacon bits.
- Bake 50 min. or until set and golden.

129. Low Carb Veggie Quiche Recipe

Serving: 4 | Prep: | Cook: 30mins | Ready in:

Ingredients

- 10   eggs, beaten
- 1   green pepper chopped
- 1   red pepper chopped
- 1   Medium onion Chopped

- 1 zuchini chopped
- 2 ts parsley flakes
- 1 ts oregano
- salt and pepper to taste
- 2 c Diced precooked chicken, or turkey sausage
- 2 tb onion flakes
- 2 ts dried chili pepper flakes
- 1/2 ts garlic powder

Direction

- Preheat oven to 350 degrees.
- Spray an 8 inch pan with non-stick spray.
- Combine ingredients in a bowl.
- Pour mixture into pan.
- Cook for 30 minutes.
- Serve! I like mine topped with salsa and cheese.

130.   Market Fresh Crustless Quiche Recipe

Serving: 4 | Prep: | Cook: 40mins | Ready in:

Ingredients

- 7 eggs
- 2 tbsp whole wheat flour
- 2-3 tbsp bread crumbs
- 1/4 tsp Magic baking powder
- 3 tbsp plain organic yogurt
- 1/4-1/3 cup of grated cheddar cheese
- 1/4 cup organic smoked ham (diced)
- 1 tbsp butter (some to grease the pan with too)
- 2-3 garlic scape (if you cannot find these then use a small clove of garlic)
- 2 market fresh baby green peppers
- 1 small tomato
- salt
- pepper
- 2 generous tbsp hickory smoked paprika

Direction

- Cut up the scape into little pieces.
- Sauté scape in butter and salt until for 5 minutes.
- Meanwhile...
- Cut up the peppers/tomatoes/grate the cheese
- After five minutes add in half of the peppers to the sauté pan (cook until scape is very soft - another 10 minutes or so).
- Meanwhile...
- Preheat the oven to 350 F.
- In a medium sized mixing bowl:
- Mix eggs.
- Blend in flour, powder, and bread crumbs (I used a hand mixer here).
- Mix in cheese/salt/pepper/paprika.
- Dice the ham.
- Add ham, raw peppers, tomatoes and your sauté mixture (once it is soft enough) to the egg mixture.
- Now - all of your friends are in the mixing bowl.
- Pour them all into a nice 8-10 inch greased square glass casserole dish.
- Bake for about 40 minutes until it's all crispy and a toothpick comes out dry.
- (One cool idea is to put these into a muffin tray for mini quiches).
- (Another cool idea is to add some extra breadcrumbs and cheese on top).

131.   Maryland Crab Quiche Recipe

Serving: 6 | Prep: | Cook: 50mins | Ready in:

Ingredients

- 1 prepared pie shell
- 8 oz lump crab meat
- 1/8 cup finely chopped sweet onion
- 1 (10 3/4 oz) can cream of chicken soup
- 1/2 cup whipping cream
- 1 cup egg beaters

- 1 cup grated mild cheddar cheese
- 1 Tb Old Bay Seasoning

Direction

- Preheat oven to 420 F.
- Spray a disposable pie plate with PAM with flour. Layer in the prepared pie shell and trim the excess from the rim of the plate.
- Bake the pie shell for 10 minutes.
- In a medium bowl, mix the chicken soup, whipping cream, and prepared egg mix. In a second bowl, clean the crab meat, removing any shell fragments, then stir in the Old Bay.
- When the pie shell begins to crust, remove from the oven and add the seasoned crab meat, the onion, and the grated cheddar. Pour the egg/soup mixture over the top.
- Reduce the oven temperature to 320 F. Place the quiche in the oven and cook for 50 minutes, or until a fork inserted into the middle of the quiche can be remove cleanly. By this time the surface should be turning brown.
- Allow to cool before serving.

132. Medieval Lombardy Quiche Recipe

Serving: 4 | Prep: | Cook: 25mins | Ready in:

Ingredients

- 2 cups thick cream
- 3 eggs plus 2 yolks
- 4 tbsp raw beef marrow chopped
- ½ cup dates, pitted and minced
- ½ cup prunes, pitted and minced
- 9" bakery shell, prebaked
- 2 tbsp parsley, finely chopped

Direction

- Heat the cream, but do not boil.

- Beat the eggs and the extra yolks in a bowl then pour in the hot cream, beating as you do. Arrange the marrow, dates and prunes in the pastry shell and pour in the custard. Stir in the parsley. Bake at 350 degrees for 25 minutes.

133. Mini Quiches Recipe

Serving: 8 | Prep: | Cook: 60mins | Ready in:

Ingredients

- Dough
- 2 cups all pusposeflour
- 1 teaspoon salt
- ¾ cup shortenng or butter
- 5 to 6tablespoons cold water
- Filling
- 3 large eggs
- 1cup cream
- 1cup milk
- salt , pepper and nutmeg
- 1 chopped green onion
- ½ cup sliced mushroms
- bacon , chopped and roasted
- ¼ cup grated parmesan cheese

Direction

- Dough for Pie Crust
- Preheat oven at 375 F.
- In food processor with knife blade attached, measure flour, shortening and salt. Process 1 to 2 seconds until mixture form fine crumbs. Add cold water, process 1, to 2 seconds until dough forms on blades. Remove dough rom bowl; with hands, shape dough into ball.
- Line each pie pan and bake for about 15 - 20 minutes.
- Filling
- While crust is baking, sauté the onion, mushrooms and add bacon.
- Spoon to fill each mini pie crust.
- In the blender mix eggs, cream, milk, salt, pepper and nutmeg.

- Pour over each mini quiche and spread grated Parmesan cheese over each one.
- Bake for about 25 – 30 minutes and ready!
- Serve warm.

134. Mini Chicken And Corn Self Crusting Quiches Recipe

Serving: 6 | Prep: | Cook: 25mins | Ready in:

Ingredients

- 4 eggs,beaten
- 3/4 c milk
- 1/4 c self raising flour
- 1 pkt cheese,onion and herb sauce mix
- 1/2 cup grated cheese
- 1/4 c fresh chopped parsley
- 3/4 c corn kernels
- 150g cooked chicken,shredded

Direction

- Preheat oven to 200C.
- Line 6 jumbo muffin pans with baking paper.
- Whisk together eggs and milk, add remaining ingredients and mix till just combined.
- Pour into the muffin pans and bake 20-25 mins or until the centre is firm.
- Allow to cool before removing from pan.
- Goes nice with a nice salsa.

135. Mini Crustless Quiche Recipe

Serving: 4 | Prep: | Cook: 14mins | Ready in:

Ingredients

- 4 slices of prosciutto, very thinly sliced!
- 4 eggs, beaten
- 1/4 low-fat ricotta cheese

- 1 slice American cheese (2% or skim milk cheese would be best)
- 1 tbsp shredded parmesan cheese
- salt and pepper to taste (I also put in a bit of garlic powder - optional)
- *note: prosciutto is very salty on its own and you do not need much added salt in this recipe. In fact, you might want to skip salt altogether and just salt the finished product if it's needed

Direction

- Spray 4 ramekins with cooking spray.
- In the bottom of each ramekin, loosely pile one slice of prosciutto in each ramekin.
- In a medium bowl, beat the 4 eggs and ricotta cheese together, season with salt and pepper to taste.
- Pour mixture evenly over the prosciutto in the ramekins.
- Tear apart and distribute bits of the American cheese among all 4 ramekins and top with parmesan cheese and one last bit of fresh cracked black pepper on top.
- Bake in a pre-heated 350 degree oven for about 13-15m or until toothpick comes out clear. Allow to rest for a couple of minutes. They should pop right out of the ramekin since you sprayed them first!

136. Mini Mushroom Sausage Quiches Recipe

Serving: 12 | Prep: | Cook: 30mins | Ready in:

Ingredients

- 8 ounces turkey breakfast sausage, removed from casing and crumbled into small pieces
- 1 teaspoon extra-virgin olive oil
- 8 ounces mushrooms, sliced
- 1/4 cup sliced scallions
- 1/4 cup shredded swiss cheese
- 1 teaspoon freshly ground pepper

- 5 eggs
- 3 egg whites
- 1 cup 1% milk

Direction

- Position rack in center of oven; preheat to 325°F.
- Coat a non-stick muffin tin generously with cooking spray
- Heat a large non-stick skillet over medium-high heat.
- Add sausage and cook until golden brown, 6 to 8 minutes.
- Transfer to a bowl to cool.
- Add oil to the pan.
- Add mushrooms and cook, stirring often, until golden brown, 5 to 7 minutes.
- Transfer mushrooms to the bowl with the sausage.
- Let cool for 5 minutes.
- Stir in scallions, cheese and pepper.
- 3. Whisk eggs, egg whites and milk in a medium bowl.
- Divide the egg mixture evenly among the prepared muffin cups. Sprinkle a heaping tablespoon of the sausage mixture into each cup.
- 4. Bake until the tops are just beginning to brown, 25 minutes.
- Let cool on a wire rack for 5 minutes.
- Place a rack on top of the pan, flip it over and turn the quiches out onto the rack.
- Turn upright and let cool completely.

---

137.   Mini Quiches Recipe

Serving: 812 | Prep: | Cook: 30mins | Ready in:

Ingredients

- Ready made pie crust
- egg Custard:
- coarse salt and freshly ground pepper
- 1/2 cup milk

- 1/2 cup heavy cream
- 2 large eggs
- 1 large egg yolk
- Pinch of freshly grated nutmeg
- all-purpose flour, for work surface
- Filling Option 1: Spinach-mushroom-Feta
- Half a bag of fresh spinach
- 1 small onion
- 1-2 cups of chopped mushrooms
- 1 tablespoon olive oil
- 1 small container of feta cheese
- Filling Option 2: red pepper-Artichoke-goat cheese
- 1 red pepper
- 1 can of artichokes
- 1 small container of goat cheese

Direction

- Preheat oven to 375 degrees. Prepare filling (see below)
- In a medium bowl, whisk together milk, heavy cream, eggs, yolk, and nutmeg. Season with salt and pepper. Set aside.
- On a lightly floured surface, roll out pie crust to slightly less than 1/8-inch thick. Using a 2 3/4-inch round cutter (I used a soup can), cut out 24 rounds. Fit rounds into a 24-cup non-stick mini muffin tin. Divide half of the cheese, evenly between the lined cups. Top with filling. Divide milk mixture evenly between cups. Sprinkle with remaining cheese.
- Bake until puffed and golden brown, about 30 minutes. Remove from oven and immediately remove quiches from muffin tin and transfer to a wire rack. Serve warm or at room temperature.
- Filling 1:
- Season and sauté coarsely chopped spinach, diced onion, and chopped mushrooms in oil until cooked (5-10 minutes). Let cool before adding to egg mixture.
- Filling 2:
- Chop red pepper finely, and drain artichokes and chop finely.

138.   Mini Sausage Quiches Appetizers Recipe

Serving: 24 | Prep: | Cook: 10mins | Ready in:

Ingredients

- 1 sheet frozen puff pastry, thawed but unfolded
- 1/2 pound bulk pork country sausage, hot or mild or italian sausage
- 1/4 cup finely minced sweet onion
- 1/4 cup finely diced sweet red bell pepper
- 1 clove finely minced garlic
- 4 ounces cream cheese (1/2 large block), at room temperature
- 1/8 tsp dry mustard powder
- 1/4 tsp ground sage
- 1/4 tsp ground thyme
- 1/4 tsp onion powder
- 1/2 tsp salt
- Dash of hot sauce, to taste
- Dash worcestershire sauce
- 2 eggs
- Shredded gruyere or swiss cheese

Direction

- Preheat oven to 400 degrees F. Grease mini-muffin pans.
- On a lightly floured board, place unfolded thawed puff pastry sheet and roll out into a rectangle 12 x 14 inches and about 1/8-inch thick. Using a 2-1/2-inch biscuit cutter, cut 24 rounds. Fit rounds into mini-muffin cups.
- Gently sauté sausage, sweet onion, red bell pepper, and garlic together until meat is no longer pink, breaking it up as you go. Drain off fat and cool to room temperature. Place 1/2 to 1 tablespoon sausage mixture into each pastry cup.
- Blend cream cheese, dry mustard, sage, thyme, onion powder, salt, hot sauce, and Worcestershire sauce until smooth. Beat in eggs, one at a time, just until incorporated.

- Spoon egg and cheese mixture over sausage in each cup. Top with a sprinkling of Gruyere or Swiss cheese
- Bake 10 minutes until puffed and golden. Serve warm.

139.   Mini Shrimp Quiches Appetizers Recipe

Serving: 24 | Prep: | Cook: 10mins | Ready in:

Ingredients

- sheet frozen puff pastry, thawed but unfolded
- 8 ounces frozen baby shrimp, thawed and patted dry (if using canned, rinse and drain)
- 4 ounces cream cheese (1/2 large block), at room temperature
- 1/8 tsp dry mustard powder
- 1/4 tsp dill weed
- 1/4 tsp garlic powder
- 1/4 tsp onion powder
- 1/2 tsp salt
- 1/2 tsp soy sauce
- 2 eggs
- 1/8 cup chopped chives
- Shredded gruyere or swiss cheese

Direction

- Preheat oven to 400 degrees F. Grease mini-muffin pans.
- On a lightly floured board, place unfolded thawed puff pastry sheet and roll out into a rectangle about 12 x 14 inches and 1/8-inch thick. Using a 2-1/2-inch biscuit cutter, cut 24 rounds. Fit rounds into mini-muffin cups. Place 1 or 2 baby shrimp into each cup.
- Blend cream cheese, dry mustard, dill weed, garlic powder, onion powder, salt, and soy sauce until smooth. Beat in eggs, one at a time, just until incorporated. Fold in chopped chives.

- Spoon egg and cheese mixture over shrimp in each cup. Top with a sprinkling of Gruyere or Swiss cheese.
- Bake 10 minutes until puffed and golden. Serve warm.
- May be baked ahead and frozen. Reheat in a 350-degree F. oven for 15 to 20 minutes.

140. Mini Wonton Quiche Recipe

Serving: 24 | Prep: | Cook: 13mins | Ready in:

Ingredients

- 4 eggs
- 1 ounce finely chopped lean cooked ham(about 3 tablespoons)
- 2 tablespoons chopped green onion with tops
- 2 tablespoons chopped sweet pepper
- 1 tablespoon flour
- cooking spray
- 24 (31/4 x 3 inch) wonton wrapper
- sweet and sour sauce, optional
- hot mustard, optional

Direction

- In medium bowl, beat together eggs, ham, onions, pepper and flour until blended. Set aside. Evenly coat 24 miniature muffin cups (13/4 x 3/4 -inch) with spray. Gently press 1 wrapper into each cup, allowing ends to extend above edges of cup. Spoon about 1/2 tablespoon egg mixture into each wrapper-lined cup.
- Bake in preheated 350 degree oven until knife inserted near centre comes out clean, about 12 to 15 minutes. Serve with sauce and or mustard, if desired.

141. Mini Quiche Recipe

Serving: 12 | Prep: | Cook: 25mins | Ready in:

Ingredients

- Crust: 1 cup flour
- 3 oz. cream cheese
- 1/2 cup butter
- Filling: 1/2 cup chopped onion
- 1 Tbsp. olive oil
- 1/2 cup sour cream
- 1 egg, slightly beaten
- 1/2 cup swiss cheese
- 1/4 tsp salt
- dash pepper

Direction

- Crust: Mix the flour, cheese and butter tog. Chill for 1 hr. Roll into 12 balls, each for 1 crust.
- Filling: Sauté the onions in the oil. Cool.
- Add the sour cream, egg, Swiss cheese, salt and pepper.
- Shape little crust in 12 mini-cupcake tins.
- Add filling.
- Bake 350 degrees for 25 to 30 minutes.

142. Mixed Vegetable Quiche Recipe

Serving: 4 | Prep: | Cook: 20mins | Ready in:

Ingredients

- 1 (9-inch) refrigerated pie crust
- 1 (10-ounce) package frozen chopped spinach, thawed and drained
- 1 cup cooked stir-fried vegetables
- 1 cup part-skim ricotta cheese
- 3/4 cup grated Cheddar
- 1/4 cup low fat milk
- 2 eggs, lightly beaten
- 2 teaspoons Dijon mustard

- 1 teaspoon dried oregano
- 1/2 teaspoon salt
- 1/4 teaspoon ground black pepper
- 1 tablespoon grated Parmesan

Direction

- Preheat oven to 375 degrees F.
- Press pie crust into the bottom and up the sides of a 9-inch, removable-bottom tart pan (or 9-inch pie pan). Set aside.
- In a large bowl, combine spinach, stir-fried vegetables and place on top of uncooked crust. In another bowl combine ricotta, cheddar, milk, eggs, Dijon, oregano, salt, and black pepper. Mix well. Spoon cheese mixture on top of vegetable mixture in prepared pie crust and top with Parmesan.
- Bake 20 minutes, until a knife inserted

- Cook the bacon until it is crisp, remove it from the pan and set it aside, then drain the fat while reserving 1 tablespoon of it in the pan.
- Add the onion and gently cook it until it is tender, but is not browned.
- In a bowl, combine the eggs, light cream or half & half, salt, and pepper.
- Crumble or roughly chop the bacon to your preference.
- Place the pie shell in a pie plate.
- Place the bacon, onion, and cheese in the bottom if the pie shell/crust, then pour the egg mixture over.
- Bake in the preheated 375 degree F oven for about 45 minutes, or until the quiche is firm and lightly browned.
- Let rest for 5 minutes, then serve immediately.
- I recommend using my Mom's Oil Crust Pie Shell recipe, too! :) Moms Oil Crust Pie Shell

---

143.   Moms French Cheese Pie Quiche Lorraine Recipe

Serving: 6 | Prep: | Cook: 45mins | Ready in:

Ingredients

- 1 unbaked 9-inch pie shell
- 6 slices bacon, cooked until crisp and crumbled (or roughly chopped)
- 3/4 cup chopped sweet onions (about 1 medium onion)
- 1 1/4 cups grated cheddar cheese (original recipe calls for swiss cheese)
- 1/4 cup grated parmesan cheese (which Mom omits, but I like)
- 3 eggs, beaten
- 1 1/2 cups light cream or half-and-half
- 1/2 teaspoon salt
- 1/4 teaspoon fresh ground black pepper

Direction

- Preheat oven to 375 degrees F.

---

144.   Monterey Chicken And Rice Quiche Recipe

Serving: 6 | Prep: | Cook: 32mins | Ready in:

Ingredients

- 4 boneless, skinless chicken tenderloins, cut into 1-inch pieces
- 13/4 cups water
- 1 box UNCLE BENS COUNTRY INN, chicken & vegetable rice
- 1 cup frozen mixed vegetables
- 1 9-inch deep dish ready to use pie crust
- 3 eggs
- 1/2 cup milk
- 1/2 cup shredded monterey jack cheese.

Direction

- Heat oven to 400 degrees.
- In large skillet, combined chicken, water, rice, contents of seasoning packet, and frozen vegetables, Bring to boil, Cover; reduce heat

and simmer 10 minutes, spoon mixture into pie crust.

- In small bowl, beat eggs and milk, pour over rice mixture in pie crust, Top with cheese, Bake for 30 to 35 minutes, or until knife inserted in center comes out clean.

145. Morel Quiche Recipe

Serving: 6 | Prep: | Cook: 40mins | Ready in:

Ingredients

- 1 Pound morels
- 1/4 Pound cooked bacon
- 1/2 Cup chopped onions
- 1/2 Cup chopped green peppers
- 1-1/2 Cups shredded (baby) swiss cheese
- 1-1/2 Cups milk
- 1 Cup Bisquick
- 3 eggs
- 1 Teaspoon salt (to taste)
- 1/4 Teaspoon pepper

Direction

- Preheat oven to 400 degrees. In a 10-inch, lightly coat pan with butter.
- Mix bacon, mushrooms, onion, green pepper and cheese in a medium-sized bowl add milk, eggs, Bisquick, salt and pepper, beat until smooth.
- Pour into pan.
- Bake 35-40 minutes or until inserted toothpick comes out clean.

146. Mozzarella Quiche Recipe

Serving: 6 | Prep: | Cook: 45mins | Ready in:

Ingredients

- 1 unbaked 9 inch pie shell
- 4 eggs
- 2 cups shredded mozzarella cheese
- 1/4 cup canned mild green or red chili peppers
- 1 clove garlic minced
- 1 tsp dried basil or oregano
- 2 cups cream
- 1 cup half and half
- salt and pepper
- paprika

Direction

- Place cheese on bottom of pie crust.
- Mix together remaining ingredients and pour over cheese.
- Sprinkle with paprika.
- Bake 375 till puffed and golden about 50 minutes or custard is set and jiggles.
- Cool to warm and cut.
- Freezes well and reheats well in the oven.

147. Mushroom And Broccoli Quiche Recipe

Serving: 6 | Prep: | Cook: 75mins | Ready in:

Ingredients

- 1 (10-ounce) box frozen chopped broccoli pieces, thawed and drained
- 1 (8-ounce) carton fresh sliced mushrooms
- 1 (9-inch) frozen deep dish prepared piecrust
- 1 medium onion, diced
- 1 - 2 garlic cloves, minced
- 4 - 5 eggs
- 1 cup liquid non-dairy creamer
- a good handful of shredded swiss cheese or 3/4 to 1 cup
- Note: You can omit the cheese - it's your choice
- 2 Tablespoons flour
- a dash of salt and grated black pepper

- NOTE: Sometimes I like to bake the pie crust for approximately 10 -12 minutes before adding the ingredients. It's up to you.

Direction

- Preheat oven to 375° F.
- Gently sauté mushrooms, onions and garlic in a tiny amount of olive oil.
- Arrange mushrooms, onions and broccoli in piecrust.
- In a bowl, place eggs and non-dairy creamer and beat.
- Add shredded Swiss cheese, flour, salt and pepper and mix to combine.
- Pour mixture over vegetables.
- Bake at 375° for 1 hour to 1 hour and 15 minutes, until mixture is set.
- Cut into wedge-shaped pieces and serve warm.
- NOTE:
- Cover the quiche loosely with aluminum foil if the center is not quite set and the crust is browning too quickly.

148.   Mushroom Asparagus Quiche

Serving: 0 | Prep: | Cook: | Ready in:

Ingredients

- 1 tube (8 ounces) refrigerated crescent rolls
- 2 teaspoons prepared mustard
- 1-1/2 pounds fresh asparagus, trimmed and cut into 1/2-inch pieces
- 1 medium onion, chopped
- 1/2 cup sliced fresh mushrooms
- 1/4 cup butter, cubed
- 2 large eggs, lightly beaten
- 2 cups shredded part-skim mozzarella cheese
- 1/4 cup minced fresh parsley
- 1/2 teaspoon salt
- 1/2 teaspoon pepper
- 1/4 teaspoon garlic powder

- 1/4 teaspoon each dried basil, oregano and rubbed sage

Direction

- Separate crescent dough into eight triangles; place in an ungreased 9-in. pie plate with points toward the center. Press onto the bottom and up the sides to form a crust; seal perforations. Spread with mustard; set aside.
- In a large skillet, saute the asparagus, onion and mushrooms in butter until asparagus is crisp-tender. In a large bowl, combine the remaining ingredients; stir in asparagus mixture. Pour into crust.
- Bake at 375° for 25-30 minutes or until a knife inserted in the center comes out clean. Let stand for 10 minutes before cutting.
- Freeze option: Cover and freeze unbaked quiche. To use, remove from freezer 30 minutes before baking (do not thaw). Preheat oven to 375°. Place quiche on a baking sheet; cover edge loosely with foil. Bake as directed, increasing time as necessary for a knife inserted in center to come out clean.
- Nutrition Facts
- 1 piece: 272 calories, 18g fat (8g saturated fat), 84mg cholesterol, 580mg sodium, 16g carbohydrate (5g sugars, 1g fiber), 12g protein.

149.   Mushroom Quiche Recipe

Serving: 12 | Prep: | Cook: 35mins | Ready in:

Ingredients

- 1 pastry crust for 9-in pie
- 2 tablespoons butter
- 1 medium onion, thinly sliced
- 1 shallot, thinly sliced
- 1 pound assorted mushrooms, sliced - I prefer cremini
- 4 strips bacon, cooked and crumbled
- 1/2 cup milk

- 1/2 cup heavy cream
- 3 large eggs
- 2 egg yolks
- Pinch of freshly grated nutmeg
- salt and freshly ground pepper
- 6 ounces gruyere cheese, grated (1 1/2 cups)

Direction

- On a lightly floured surface, roll dough into a 12-inch circle, or, press the pastry dough into a tart pan or pie plate, pressing the dough into the corners. Transfer to fridge to chill for 30 minutes.
- Preheat oven to 350°. Line the pastry with parchment paper, wax paper, or aluminum foil, pressing into the corners and edges. Fill at least two-thirds with baking weights -I use dried beans.
- Bake first for 10 minutes, remove from oven and let cool a few minutes. Carefully remove parchment paper and weights. Poke the bottom of the pie pan with the tongs of a fork and return to oven and bake an additional 10 minutes or until lightly golden. Transfer to a wire rack to cool while making filling.
- Heat butter in a large non-stick skillet over medium high heat. Add onions and shallots, and cook, stirring, until brown - we want them to caramelize a bit. Add mushrooms. Cook, stirring frequently, until mushrooms first release their liquid and then liquid evaporates and mushrooms are dark golden brown, 8 to 10 minutes.
- Place tart pan on a baking sheet. Sprinkle half the cheese evenly over the bottom of the crust. Spread mushroom-onion mixture over the cheese, sprinkle the crumbled bacon on top and then top with remaining cheese.
- In a medium bowl, whisk together milk, cream, eggs and egg yolks. Season with nutmeg, salt, and pepper. Pour over the filling, making sure it spreads out and covers everything.
- Bake until just set in the center, 30 to 35 minutes. Cool on a wire rack for about 10 minutes before slicing.

My Easy Quiche Recipe

Serving: 8 | Prep: | Cook: 45mins | Ready in:

Ingredients

- 1-9" pie shell
- 6 eggs, beaten
- 1 pound mozzerella cheese, sharp or provolone. Mix and make any cheses for this.
- 1 cup of vegies (I usually use grated zucchini)
- 1/2 cup onion, sliced thin in strips.
- To taste: salt, pepper, parsley, spices you wish
- ANYTHING GOES!
- I have even used left over grilled veggies.

Direction

- Okay, this is simple.
- Place veggies in pie shell.
- Add cheese.
- Pour over eggs add spices to eggs or top it on the pie.
- Or you can mix it all together and pour into shell.
- Bake at 350 for around 45 minutes. Check if butter knife comes out clean it is done. Could be more or less time.
- Enjoy

151. **No Crust Smoked Salmon Quiche Recipe**

Serving: 6 | Prep: | Cook: 45mins | Ready in:

Ingredients

- 4 eggs, beaten
- 1/2 cup melted butter
- 1/2 cup buttermilk baking mix
- 1-1/2 cups milk

- 1/2 cups sharp cheddar cheese, grated
- 1/2 cups swiss cheese, grated
- 3/4 cups chopped or flaked smoked salmon

Direction

- Beat the eggs, butter, baking mix and milk together with a wire whisk. Butter a large pie pan or quiche pan. Pour in the egg mixture. Dot the mixture with the cheese and salmon, pressing into the egg mixture if necessary to submerge the cheese and salmon. Bake in a preheated oven at 350 degrees for 45 minutes.
- Cut into wedges to serve.

152.   Northwestern Salmon Quiche Recipe

Serving: 8 | Prep: | Cook: 60mins | Ready in:

Ingredients

- 1 cup all-purpose flour
- 1 cup grated parmesan cheese, divided
- 1/4 cup chopped hazelnuts (walnuts, almonds, or pecans)
- 1/2 teaspoon salt
- 1/4 teaspoon paprika
- 6 tablespoons extra-virgin olive oil
- 1/2 cup milk
- 3 eggs, beaten
- 1 cup sour cream
- 1/4 cup mayonnaise
- 1 tablespoon finely chopped fresh chives
- 1/4 teaspoon Colgin's Smoke flavoring
- 1/4 teaspoon salt
- 1/4 teaspoon pepper
- 1 1/2 to 2 cups cooked salmon, (ok to used canned) flaked and all skin and bones removed
- sour cream & fresh dill for garnish

Direction

- Preheat oven to 400 degrees. In a medium bowl, combine flour, 3/4 cup parmesan cheese, hazelnuts, salt, paprika, and olive oil. Press mixture onto bottom and sides of a 10-inch pie plate or quiche pan. Bake for 10 minutes; remove from oven and reduce oven temperature to 325 degrees.
- In a large bowl, combine milk, eggs, sour cream, mayonnaise, chives, liquid smoke, salt, and pepper. Stir in flaked salmon and remaining 1/2 cup parmesan cheese. Pour mixture into baked crust. Bake approximately 45 to 50 minutes or until a knife inserted in the center comes out clean. Remove from oven and let cool 12 to 15 minutes.
- To serve, spread a thin layer of sour cream over the top. Cut into wedges and serve.
- Makes 4 dinner-size servings and 6 to 8 lunch or appetizer servings.

153.   Nouveau Quiche Recipe

Serving: 6 | Prep: | Cook: 70mins | Ready in:

Ingredients

- 1.) 1 deep dish pie shell
- 2.) 1 1/2 cup Shredded Kraft Mexican Style 4 cheese blend. It has cheddar, jack, adero and quesadilla cheeses if you dont have access to the exact same thing.
- 3.) 1/2 cup asiago, parmesean, romano cheese blend.
- 4.) 8oz plain yogurt/water mixture...mix yogurt with water until the consistency of heavy cream. Use low fat if you want to, or use heavy cream if you prefer. Should be about 4-6 ounces of yogurt and the rest water. Whisk with a fork to blend it well.
- 5.) 4 Large eggs
- 6.) 6 thinly sliced medium sized mushrooms
- 7.) 3/4 cup julienne zucchini
- 8.) 3/4 cup of cooked chicken chunks, cooked shrimp or lobster, or artichoke chunks. I think

if u used artichoke bottoms instead of baby artichokes it would be better.

- 9.) 1/2 tsp. black pepper
- 10.) 1/2 tsp nutmeg
- 11.) 1 tsp sea salt
- 12.) 1 tsp finely diced fresh, orange habanero pepper. This can be increased to taste. At this amount, you wont feel the heat, so if you prefer double it and make it a more intense flavor.
- 13.) 1 clove garlic, very thinly sliced or crushed.
- 14.) Fresh cilantro, asiago cheese blend and Sriracha (Rooster) sauce for garnish.

Direction

- 1.) Bake pie shell on 250 F for 20 min or so. Poke holes in it with a fork to prevent bubbles from forming. It should be light golden brown.
- 2.) Turn oven up to 325 F when pie shell is out.
- 3.) Blend wet ingredients in large bowl, beating in eggs one at a time.
- 4.) Mix in cheeses.
- 5.) Stir in dry ingredients.
- 6.) Pour mixture into pie crust, don't worry if the crust is hot still.
- 7.) Bake at 325 for 1 hour.
- 8.) Check on quiche, you may find it is not completely dry in the middle on top like I did. To solve this problem, I turned the oven up to 400 F and let it sit in there for about 7-10 more min, and then the top was perfect.
- 9.) Serve this quiche hot, it is much better this way...cool for about 10 min and then slice while hot from the oven.
- 10.) Serve each slice with a sprig of fresh cilantro, a stripe of rooster sauce and sprinkle a little asiago cheese blend on top.
- 11.) This goes great with a Caesar salad.

Serving: 3 | Prep: | Cook: 1hours | Ready in:

Ingredients

- For the Crust
- * 1 cup Wholewheat flour
- * 1/2 cup oats
- * 1/3 cup olive oil/melted butter
- * 1/2 tsp. salt
- * 1/2 tsp. baking powder
- * 1/2 cup water/milk
- For the Filling
- * 1 cup of shredded spinach
- * 1/2 cup of color bell pepper
- * 1 onion
- * 2 cloves of garlic
- * 1 tsp red chilly flakes
- * 1/2 tsp dry herbs
- * 1/2 cup tofu
- * 2 tbsp olive oil
- * salt as desired
- * 1/2 tsp of fresh black pepper
- * 1/2 cup of cheddar cheese

Direction

- For the Crust: Slightly dry roast the oats for a few minutes and grind it along with all the dry ingredients. Take the ground mix in a large vessel and make a well in it. Add the olive oil or butter into it. Rub the whole flour mix with light hand till it resembles bread crumbs.
- Add water or milk as a binding agent. Make a hard dough, increase the quantity of liquid if you are not getting a firm dough.
- Take a pie dish and grease it with oil. Roll out the above made dough into a big circle and spread it in the dish. Trim the extra dough which is coming out of the dish. Peirce the pastry shell with fork to ensure a crispy bake.
- Bake the pastry shell for about 10-15 minutes at 230°C till the crust is baked and is golden brown from outside. You can blind bake the crust for better results.

- Peel and slice onion, dice the capsicum. Wash and shred the spinach. Crush the garlic cloves or dice it finely. Heat oil in a wok and sauté the sliced onion & the crushed garlic.
- Add the sliced capsicum and cook for 1 minute on medium heat. Add the shredded spinach & salt and cook for another 1 minute. Take the filling out from the stove and cool it a little.
- The liquid you see in the picture above is the water released while cooking the spinach. Don't worry it will all be taken care of by the oven!
- Crumble the Tofu and mix it with the 1 tbsp. of milk and add it to the cooked spinach mix. Grate the cheese.
- Assembling the Quiche: Pour the cooked spinach mix over the pre baked tart shell. Sprinkle the chili flakes and crushed pepper over the spread. And lastly add the grated cheese on top of the assembled Quiche.
- Bake the Quiche for 40-50 minutes at 190°C or till done. Cool it for 10 -15 minutes before slicing the Quiche.
- Quiche is one dish, which looks complicated but is quite easy to bake. Am sure you will love this, once you get to bake one for yourself. And what better way to add wholegrain and veggies in your kids' menu than a decadent vegetable Quiche!

155. One Dish Crab Quiche Recipe

Serving: 8 | Prep: | Cook: 60mins |Ready in:

Ingredients

- 1 refrigerated fluted pie crust
- 1/4 cup finely chopped vidalia onion
- 1/4 cup finely diced red bell pepper
- 1 cup chopped blanched drained fresh chard
- 1 cup whole milk
- 3 eggs

- 1 cup diced swiss cheese
- 8 ounces cream cheese softened and cut into 1/2" squares
- 1/2 pound fresh crab meat
- 1/2 teaspoon paprika

Direction

- Line pie plate with pie crust.
- In a large bowl thoroughly whisk the eggs.
- Add and mix together all other items listed above except crabmeat.
- Lastly stir in gently the crabmeat and pour into pie dish.
- Bake in preheated oven at 350 for 1 hour.
- Remove and dust with paprika and serve.

156. Otterpond Shrimp Quiche Recipe

Serving: 12 | Prep: | Cook: 45mins |Ready in:

Ingredients

- ---- SHRIMP BOIL ----
- 1 lb shrimp
- 4 cups water
- 1/4 cup Old Bay Seasoning
- 1 tsp apple cider vinegar
- 1 tsp tabasco
- 1 tsp salt
- 2 pie shells - pre-baked
- 4 slices Turkey Bacon, cooked
- 1 cup mixed minced onion, red bell pepper and poblano pepper
- 1/4 cup reserved shrimp boil water
- 5 eggs
- 1/2 cup evaporated milk
- 2 tbsp butter
- 2 tbsp Key Lime Curd (link to recipe below)
- 2 cup Swiss cheese, finely shredded

Direction

- COOK THE SHRIMP

- Get the water boiling and add the vinegar, tabasco and salt.
- Put the Old Bay Seasoning in a coffee filter and staple it shut to make a bag. Toss the bag in the boiling water.
- When you have a good hard boil toss in the shrimp. When the turn pink and float to the top they are done.
- NOTE: Reserve a cup of the shrimp boil water to sauté the vegetables in.
- Drain the shrimp and run cold water over them to stop the cooking.
- Sauté the minced onions and peppers in about 1/4 cup of the shrimp boil water until well softened.
- Whisk together the egg, milk, butter and key lime curd. When well beaten fold in the vegetables.
- NOTE: Link to Key Lime Curd recipe. But you can also buy lemon curd in most groceries.
- Key Lime Curd
- You have enough ingredients to make two quiches. So halves on everything.
- Into the pie shell first layer of shrimp, top shrimp with a good layer of cheese, then pour on the egg and vegetable mix.
- Preheat oven to 350 and bake for about 45 minutes or until egg is firm.

---

157. Passover Quiche 101 Recipe

Serving: 4 | Prep: | Cook: 35mins | Ready in:

Ingredients

- BASIC QUICHE-plain yet delicious!
- 6 sheets of crumbled-up matzoh (matzah)
- 6 eggs, beaten
- 1 cup of grated cheddar or monterey jack (you can try all of your favorite cheeses including swiss or gruyere)
- 1 Tb. butter or margarine to brush over the top before baking.

- ------------------------------
- QUICHE VARIETIES:
- *Mushroom Quiche*
- 1 cup sauteed (in butter) sliced mushrooms, gruyere cheese, cheddar or jack cheese (add onions or garlic if you wish)
- *Zuchinni Quiche*
- Add 1 cup pre-cooked zuchinni and use monterey jack cheese or swiss
- *potato Quiche*
- 1 cup of sliced or chopped cooked potatoes with cheddar cheese
- OR Swiss
- *Tomato Quiche*
- Add 1/2 cup chopped fresh tomatoes or canned, 1/2 cup parmesan cheese, 1/2 cup mozzarella cheese (You can use a small can of Rotel tomatoes and chiles or 1/2 of your favorite salsa (if you use salsa or a spicy tomato mix, use monterey jack cheese!)
- *spinach Quiche*
- Add 1 cup fresh spinach leaves or 1/2 cup cooked spinach with 1 cup of gruyere, jack, cheddar or swiss cheese and sprinkle top with parmesan. (If you place fresh spinach leaves over the top of the quiche and then spread with butter, you'll have a lovely -looking quiche!)
- *Black olive and green onion Quiche*
- Add 1/2 cup whole olives and 1/2 cup chopped green scallions. Use Jack or white cheddar.
- *asparagus Quiche*
- Add 1 can of asparagus, drained and chopped or 12 fresh, chopped and lightly steamed asparagus. Use gruyere or swiss cheese.
- *Artichoke Quiche*
- 1 thawed box of artichoke hearts, sauteed in butter and chopped well. I love monterey jack in this recipe.
- ***
- For a sweet quiche, try these recipes!
- *coconut Quiche*

- Add 1 cup of sweetened coconut, 1/4 cup chocolate chips and sprinkle with powdered sugar when cooled. (Its almost a pie!)
- You can pour melted chocolate over the top or add a ganache topping or drizzle!
- *Apple Quiche* (Try peaches, too!)
- 1 1/2 can apple pie filling or 2 fresh granny smith apples, peeled and chopped, 1 Tb cinnamon, 1/4 tsp. nutmeg, 2 Tb granulated sugar (and a few raisins or walnuts!).
- *raisin walnut Quiche *(This is so good!)
- 1/2 cup chopped walnuts
- 1 /2 cup raisins (soaked in warm wine or orange juice for 15 minutes and drained.
- 1 tsp. cinnamon
- You can add chocolate chips if you wish and sprinkle lightly with powdered sugar as soon as it comes out of the oven OR sprinkle with 1 TB of granulated sugar after you brush the top with butter before putting it into the oven. (The sugar will brown over the top. You can use brown sugar.)
- *pineapple Quiche*
- Add 1/2 cup cottage cheese and 1/2 crushed and drained pineapple. Add a few raisins if you like!

Direction

- Soak the crumbled matzoh in a small amount of warm water until it is soft.
- Blend eggs into matzoh and sprinkle lightly with salt and pepper.
- If you are adding a vegetable, do so now, stirring into the egg mixture.
- Add the cheese of your choice and blend all.
- Place into a quiche pan or pie pan, spreading evenly.
- Brush the top with butter or margarine.
- Bake for 30-40 minutes.
- For a special touch, I make these in small, individual tins so that each guest has their own quiche. You can use large cupcake paper liners or small cake liners found in restaurant supply chain stores.
- The dessert quiches can be topped with freshly-whipped cream.

158.   Paula Deens Potato Crusted Ham Quiche Recipe

Serving: 8 | Prep: | Cook: 45mins | Ready in:

Ingredients

- 1 cup Smithfield ham, fully cooked and chopped (any ham will work, except Smithfield country ham, which is too salty)
- 2 cups of potatoes, raw and shredded
- 1/4 cup onion, minced
- 1/2 cup red bell pepper, finely diced
- 1 tablespoon chives, finely chopped
- 3 eggs, separated
- salt and pepper to taste
- 3/4 cup sharp cheddar cheese, grated
- 3/4 cup smoked gouda cheese, grated
- 1 cup evaporated milk
- 1/2 teaspoon paprika
- 1/2 teaspoon salt (optional)
- 1/4 teaspoon pepper

Direction

- Preheat the oven to 375 degrees F. Spray quiche pan with non-stick cooking spray. In a medium bowl mix the potatoes, onion, pepper, chives, 1 beaten egg and salt and pepper to taste.
- Press potato mixture evenly into crust shape up the side and on the bottom of the pan and spray again.
- Bake for 15 minutes or until lightly browned on edges.
- In a mixing bowl, combine the two cheeses.
- Remove the crust from oven and layer the following: ham first, and then cheese mixture on top.
- In a bowl, beat together evaporated milk, 2 eggs, paprika, salt and pepper.
- Pour mixture on top of cheese and return to oven.

- Bake about 25-30 minutes or until a toothpick inserted into the middle of the pie comes out clean.
- Allow to cool at least five minutes.

159. Phyllo Quiches Recipe

Serving: 8 | Prep: | Cook: 15mins | Ready in:

Ingredients

- 2 packages (10 ounces each) frozen chopped spinach, thawed and squeezed to drain
- 2 cups sliced fresh mushrooms (6 ounces)
- **you can use any combination of veggies. I love onion in mine.
- ** you can add fried bacon as well.
- 2 cups milk (I often use half and half, or light or heavy cream)
- 1 teaspoon ground mustard
- 1/2 teaspoon salt
- 1/4 teaspoon ground nutmeg
- 4 eggs
- 8 frozen (thawed) phyllo sheets (18 x 14 inches)
- 4 teaspoons butter or margarine, melted
- 1/2 cup shredded mozzarella cheese (2 ounces) (I mix this into the egg mix. I often use various cheese or just swiss, havarti, sharp, provolone anything goes!)

Direction

- Heat oven to 350°F.
- Spray 10- or 12-inch skillet with cooking spray.
- Cook spinach and mushrooms in skillet over medium heat, stirring occasionally, until spinach is wilted and mushrooms are tender; remove from heat.
- Mix milk, mustard, salt, nutmeg and eggs; set aside.
- Spray eight 6-ounce custard cups with cooking spray.
- Place 1 phyllo sheet on flat surface; lightly brush with butter.

- Top with 3 phyllo sheets, brushing each with butter.
- Cut phyllo into fourths.
- Place 1 phyllo section in each custard cup.
- Repeat with remaining phyllo sheets.
- Trim overhanging edge of phyllo 1 inch from rim of cup.
- Drain spinach mixture; divide evenly among cups.
- Pour about 1/3 cup egg mixture into each cup.
- Fold edges of phyllo toward center.
- Arrange custard cups in jelly roll pan, 15 1/2x10 1/2x1 inch.
- Bake 15 to 20 minutes or until egg mixture is set.
- Sprinkle with cheese (I mix mine in the egg mixture)
- Serve immediately.
- Use your imagination or what you like. Add bacon, or sausage to the veggie mix. Cook them first of course.
- Nutmeg is a must, fresh if you have it.
- Sometimes I make a big pie.
- Oh, how I love cooking!

160. Pips Quick Quiche Recipe

Serving: 6 | Prep: | Cook: 50mins | Ready in:

Ingredients

- 4 cups frozen vegetable medley (to include broccoli, cauliflower, peppers etc) or can use cooked fresh ingredients (but it's not worth the hassle- they contain the same or less nutrients than the frozen type and you have to chop them).
- hand full cooked bacon, chopped into 1cm squares
- large hand full grated edam cheese
- 1 spring onion OR 1 red onion finely chopped
- mushrooms (if you like them!)
- 5 eggs

- 3/4 cup flour
- 1 1/2 cups milk.

Direction

- Preheat oven to 180 degrees.
- Lightly grease a 26cm pie dish.
- In a mixing bowl mix eggs, flour and milk and mix well (season with S+P if desired)
- Put the veggies (including onion and mushrooms) and the bacon into the greased dish. Sprinkle grated cheese over the top.
- Pour the egg/flour/milk mixture over the top evenly.
- Bake for 50mins or until firm to touch.

---

161.   Pizza Quiche Recipe

Serving: 8 | Prep: | Cook: 45mins | Ready in:

Ingredients

- 1 unbaked 9 inch pie shell, we did not use this
- 2 cups mozzarella cheese, shredded - we used low fat
- 1 cup cheddar cheese, shredded - again as low fat as possible
- 1 cup montererrey jack cheese, shredded - low fat also
- 3/4 cup pepperoni pieces, we made one with this and one without as I am not fond of pepperioni, we used italian sausage in mine, yes I know it has lots of fat!!
- 4 ounces mushrooms, drained - or we used fresh
- 1 tablespoon olive oil
- 1/2 cup onion, finely chopped - we used red to add color to the quiche
- 2 cloves garlic, minced
- 1 cup whole milk - we used 1 percent and it worked out fine
- 3 eggs
- 1 teaspoon italian seasoning
- -

- we also used pizza sauce with lots of veggies in it to top the quiche with before serving, the kids thought it was the cats meow! But this is just an option.

Direction

- Preheat the oven to 400 degrees f.
- Sprinkle cheeses in bottom of the pie crust.
- Tope with pepperoni and mushrooms.
- In a heavy skillet, sauté the onions and garlic in the olive oil until crisp tender.
- Spoon over the mushrooms in the pie crust.
- In a medium bowl, combine milk, eggs, and Italian seasoning until well blended and pour gently over the other stuff in the pie crust (or just the small casserole dish for us).
- Bake quiche at 400 degrees for 40 to 45 minutes or until a knife inserted near the center comes out clean. Just like any other custard.
- Let stand 10 minutes before serving.
- Slice it pretty and we served it with a little bit of pizza sauce on it and a side salad with fat free dressing. It was too good to be real!

---

162.   Pizza Rustica (Cold Cut Pie) Recipe

Serving: 0 | Prep: | Cook: 2hours | Ready in:

Ingredients

- FOR THE DOUGH:
- 6 cups all-purpose flour, plus more as needed
- 1/4 teaspoon salt
- 1 pound chilled salted butter, cut into large pieces
- 5 large eggs, beaten
- FOR THE FILLING:
- 12 ounces prosciutto, in 1/4-inch dice
- 8 ounces boiled ham, in 1/4-inch dice
- 8 ounces pepperoni, in 1/4-inch dice
- 8 ounces soppressata, in 1/4-inch dice
- 8 ounces mozzarella, in 1/4-inch dice

- 8 ounces provolone, in 1/4-inch dice
- 2 pounds ricotta
- 4 ounces grated pecorino Romano
- 4 ounces formagetto, in 1/4 - inch dice
- 8 large eggs, hard boiled, in 1/4 -inch dice
- 10 large eggs, beaten
- 1 1/2 cups spinach, cooked, chopped, and well drained (optional)
- 2 Tablespoons fresh Italian parsley, finely chopped
- 1 teaspoon pepper
- Dash of salt
- 1 large egg, beaten, for brushing crust.

Direction

- 1. For the dough: In a large bowl, whisk together 6 cups flour and the salt. Using a pastry cutter, large fork, or two knives, cut the butter into the flour until the mixture resembles coarse crumbs. Add eggs and knead for 1 minute. Add about 1 1/4 cups ice water, a little at a time, to form a cohesive dough. Knead the dough on a lightly floured surface until it forms a large smooth ball, about 5 minutes. Cover with plastic wrap and set aside for 30 minutes.
- 2. For the filling: Mix the meats, cheeses, chopped boiled eggs, spinach (if desired, Italian parsley, the 10 eggs, salt and pepper in a large bowl.
- 3. Heat oven to 350 degrees. Divide the dough into two pieces: two-thirds for the bottom crust and one-third for the top. On a lightly floured surface, roll out the larger portion of the dough into a rectangle to line the bottom and sides of a 10-by-15-inch glass baking dish, with some overhang. Add the filling and smooth it lightly. Moisten the edges of the dough with a little water.
- 4. Roll out the remaining dough to cover the top of the dish with some overhang. Trim off excess dough and crimp the edges to seal. Poke several sets of holes across the top with a fork. Bake for 45 minutes. Remove from the oven and brush top and edges with the beaten egg, then return to the oven until golden brown, another 45 minutes. Let pie cool completely before serving. Serve at room temperature.
- Yield: One 10-by-15-inch pie.

163. Potato Crusted Quiche Recipe

Serving: 8 | Prep: | Cook: 45mins |Ready in:

Ingredients

- 1 red pepper, diced
- 1/2 red onion, diced
- 2-4 cloves garlic, minced or pressed
- 1 ham steak, diced into 1/4 inch cubes
- 3 medium to large potatoes, scrubbed and grated
- 6 oz smoked gouda (or other smoked cheese), shredded
- 8 eggs
- 1 pint cream
- Jalepeno hot sauce, to taste (optional)
- salt and pepper
- 3 tbsp butter, divided

Direction

- Preheat oven to 400 degrees.
- In a 10-inch non-stick, oven proof pan, using 1 tbsp. of butter, sauté peppers and onion over medium-high heat for 5 minutes.
- Add garlic and ham steak and continue to sauté for an additional 2 minutes. Remove mixture to small bowl.
- Melt additional 1 tbsp. butter and carefully press grated potatoes into pan to form a "crust". Potatoes should come up to the lip on the pan. Dot potatoes with remaining tbsp. of butter.
- Evenly spread pepper and ham mixture over the potatoes.
- Evenly sprinkle shredded cheese over the pepper and ham mixture.

- In a medium bowl, beat eggs, cream, hot sauce (if using), salt, and pepper and pour over mixture.
- Bake in preheated oven for approx. 30 minutes, or until top is golden brown and knife inserted into the center comes out clean.
- Carefully remove from oven (handle will be HOT!!!) and allow to cool for 5 minutes. Loosen from pan using spatula, slide onto platter or cutting board, and cut into 8 wedges.

164. Potato Crust Quiche Recipe

Serving: 4 | Prep: | Cook: 60mins |Ready in:

Ingredients

- 2 cups frozen hash browns, thawed
- 1 cup of any type of yummy cheese (mozzarella may not be a good choice)
- 1/2 cup sliced mushrooms
- 2 cups broccoli florets (I like to cut the broccoli up into quite small pieces)
- 4 eggs
- 1/4 cup of milk
- 1/2 tsp each of dried thyme and onion powder
- 1/4 tsp salt
- pepper (how much you would like)
- *** You really can add whatever veggies you would prefer***

Direction

- Preheat oven to 350 degrees.
- Lightly press hash browns into a greased 9 inch pie plate to form a crust.
- Sprinkle with 1/2 cup of cheese and then top with your veggies.
- Beat eggs with a wire whisk.
- Add milk, thyme, onion powder, salt and pepper.
- Whisk until well blended.
- Pour over the hash brown crust and veggies.
- Sprinkle with remaining 1/2 cup of cheese.

- Bake 1 hour until the centre is set and the top is nice and golden.

165. Potato Bacon Quiche Recipe

Serving: 6 | Prep: | Cook: 30mins |Ready in:

Ingredients

- 8 oz bacon, cooked & crumbled
- 2 lg potatoes, peeled & cubed
- 1/4 c chopped onion
- 1/4 c chopped bell pepper
- 1 tsp salt
- 1/4 tsp pepper
- 3 eggs
- 1 c Swiss or cheddar cheese, grated
- 1 c milk
- 1/4 c biscuit mix
- 2 tbsp butter, melted

Direction

- 1. Cook bacon in skillet until browned and crisp. Remove bacon and drain on paper towel.
- 2. Pour off all but 4 tablespoons bacon fat from skillet. Cook potatoes, onion, and bell pepper in bacon fat until potatoes are tender, but not mushy, about 15 minutes. Remove from heat and stir in bacon.
- 3. Beat together eggs, cheese, milk, baking mix, butter, salt, and pepper. Pour egg mixture into greased quiche dish deep dish pie plate. Spoon potato mixture on top of eggs.
- 4. Bake at 375 degrees for 20-30 minutes or until set. To serve, cut into wedges.

166.   Potato Bacon Torte Recipe

Serving: 4 | Prep: | Cook: 2hours | Ready in:

Ingredients

- Potato-Bacon Torte
- Recipe courtesy Melissa d'Arabian and foodtv.com
- Prep Time:
- 25 min
- Inactive Prep Time:
- 30 min
- Cook Time:
- 55 min
- Level:
- Intermediate
- Serves:
- 4 servings plus leftovers
- Ingredients
- 4 strips bacon
- 3 sprigs fresh thyme
- 2/3 cup heavy cream
- 2 pie crusts, recipe follows
- 3 medium baking potatoes, peeled
- salt and freshly ground black pepper
- 1/4 cup grated gruyere cheese
- 1 egg yolk, whisked with a splash of water
- Directions
- Preheat the oven to 375 degrees F.

Direction

- In a skillet over medium heat, cook the bacon until just crispy. Drain on paper towel lined plate and set aside. Crumble the bacon when cool to the touch.
- Meanwhile, in a small saucepan, heat the thyme and cream over low heat to a bare simmer. Turn off the heat and let steep for about 5 minutes. Remove the thyme sprigs.
- Remove the pie pan from the refrigerator. Slice the potatoes in half lengthwise and then finely slice the potatoes. Working in circles, arrange the potato slices in the pie crust, stopping to season each layer with salt, pepper, and about

1/4 of the crumbled bacon. Continue layering until the pie pan is nearly full. Top with an even layer of the cheese and gently pour cream around and over the entire pie, allowing it to seep down between the potato slices. (You may not use all the cream.)

- Roll out the remaining disk of refrigerated dough. Cover the pie with the dough and crimp the edges closed. Brush the top and edges of the crust with egg wash. Make a few slits in the center of the top crust, for the steam to escape, and put the pie pan on a baking sheet. Bake the torte until the crust is browned and crispy and the potatoes are cooked through, about 50 to 60 minutes. If the crust edges get too brown, cover them with some strips of aluminum foil. Remove the pie from the oven and let rest at least 15 minutes before cutting into wedges and serving.
- Pie Crust:
- 1 cup butter (2 sticks), cubed and chilled
- 2 1/4 cups all-purpose flour
- 1 teaspoon salt
- 8 to 10 tablespoons ice water
- Put the butter, flour, and salt in the food processor, and pulse lightly just until the mixture resembles wet sand. Add the water, 1 tablespoon at a time, pulsing briefly after each spoonful of water. Keep adding water until the dough just begins to gather into larger clumps. Transfer equal amounts of the dough into 2 resealable plastic bags and pat each into a disk. Let rest in the refrigerator for at least 30 minutes. Remove 1 of the disks from the bag to a flour coated surface. Using a rolling pin, roll the dough out to a 10-inch round. Gently fit the rolled dough into a 9-inch pie pan, and refrigerate while you prepare the torte ingredients.
- Yield: 2 (9-inch) pie crusts

167. Quiche Your Choice Of Flavors Recipe

Serving: 4 | Prep: | Cook: 40mins | Ready in:

Ingredients

- 4 eggs
- 1 1/2 cup milk
- 1 1/2 cup shredded swiss cheese
- 1 T. flour
- 1/4 t. nutmeg
- 1/4 t. pepper
- 1/2 t. salt
- 1 deep dish 9" pie shell (frozen)
- ***
- Suggested added ingredients:
- 1/2 cup sliced leeks, cut finely and sautéed in butter
- 1 cup sliced mushrooms chopped and sautéed in butter
- 1/2 cup onions chopped and sliced finely sautéed in butter
- 1 cup asparagus cut in 1" pieces and steamed briefly for 4 minutes
- 1 cup broccoli florets
- bacon, ham, etc.

Direction

- Prick with fork before baking after letting pie shell thaw for 15 minutes.
- Bake pie shell at 450 degrees according to package directions for 10-15 minutes.
- Turn oven down to 350 degrees for baking quiche
- Mix flour with shredded cheese and put into pie shell.
- Add whatever other ingredients you want in the quiche (suggested ingredients above).
- Mix eggs, milk, seasonings together and pour into baked pie shell.
- Place pie pan on baking sheet and bake in the center of the oven for 35-40 minutes or until a knife inserted in center of pie comes out clean.

168. Quiche A La Liezel Recipe

Serving: 6 | Prep: | Cook: 35mins | Ready in:

Ingredients

- 2 onions
- 1 green pepper
- 12 mushrooms
- 12 peppadews (mild) - if you don't get these, a few chillies to taste
- 200 grams ham (7oz; 0.45 pound)
- 50 ml (2 heaped tablespoons + 4 teaspoons) chopped fresh parsley, or 30 ml dry (2 heaped tablespoons)
- salt and pepper
- 60 ml (1/2 cup) savoury cream cheese
- 6 eggs
- 60 ml (1/2 cup) all purpose flour
- 750 ml (3 cups) cheese, grated

Direction

- Chop onions, green pepper, mushrooms, peppadews and ham.
- Sauté in a little bit of oil until onions are soft and ham is cooked if you used raw ham.
- Stir in the parsley, salt and pepper to taste.
- Remove from heat.
- Stir in the cream cheese.
- Stir in the eggs and flour until well mixed.
- Stir in the grated cheese.
- Place in a pie dish, round or square or into muffin pans.
- Bake for 30 to 40 minutes at 150 degrees C (320 deg F) until stiff in the middle.
- Serve with rice or a salad.

169. Quiche Appetizer Recipe

Serving: 16 | Prep: | Cook: 50mins | Ready in:

Ingredients

- 2 cups cooked rice
- 1 pound cooked crumbled Italian or turkey sausage
- 3/4 stick pepperoni (cubed into small pieces)
- 1 large mozzerella cheese (cubed small)
- 5-6 eggs beaten well
- 1 cup grated cheese
- 1/2 cup well drained roasted peppers cut into small pieces

Direction

- Mix all above well and put into a greased 9 x 13 pan.
- Bake 45-50 minutes or until golden brown.
- Cut into squares and serve.

---

170.   Quiche Dinner With Prosciutto Recipe

Serving: 6 | Prep: | Cook: 1hours | Ready in:

Ingredients

- for the curst
- 2 cups flour
- 1/2 cup Butter Flavor Crisco
- 1/2 butter (very cold cut into small chunks
- 1/4 tea. salt
- 1/8 tea. pepper
- 1/2 cup ice water
- for the Quiche
- 6 eggs
- 1 cup 1% milk
- 1 cup whole milk
- 1 cup half and half
- 1 tea spoon salt or a little less (little)
- 1/2 tea spoon pepper
- 1/4 tea cayenne pepper
- 2 cloves of garlic
- 1 small onion chopped
- 1 tea spoon olive oil
- 1 small sweet poatoe
- 1 pear
- 1 cup 5 itilian cheese mix
- 1/2 cup good chedder cheese (yellow)
- 1/4 lb prosciutto or panchetta (baccon if nessary)

Direction

- For the curst: in a bowl add flour, salt and pepper mix.
- Add the Crisco and butter mix till the flour and fats are combined into different little sizes, add all at once 1/2 cup ice water mix till combined and divide in 1/2 and freeze one for latter and place one in the frig for 1/2 hr.
- Clean the pear slice and roast in the oven at 350 with a sprinkle of balsamic vinegar until just tender about 10 mi.
- Cook your onions and garlic until tender in 1 teaspoon olive oil.
- Clean the sweet potatoes and using a mandolin slice it into thin rounds.
- Roll crust by placing ample flour on your board and on top of the dough. It may be sticky (not a problem) keep working the flour into the dough until you have a round curst for you pie plate. Place the curt into you plate and crimp, lay the sweet rounds on the bottom and side, set into the fridge. Kitchen aide or mixer, break eggs add seasons milks, and mix just till mixed do not foam. Get your curst add in cheese and meat (if using prosciutto slice into long strips) pour egg in and bake at 425 for 15 mi. reduce heat to 350 for 30 mi. or until your egg is set. Remove and let cool for 1/2 hr. before serving and fan roasted pear on the top.
- NOTE: if using pancetta or bacon cook until brown and drain well remove all fat from pan except 1 table spoon and add onions and garlic until tender.

---

171.   Quiche Lorraine Recipe

Serving: 6 | Prep: | Cook: 45mins | Ready in:

Ingredients

- 1 cup bacon bits
- 1 cup (4 oz.) shredded cheddar cheese
- 1 cup (4 oz.) shredded swiss cheese
- 1 unbaked 9-inch pie shell (I prefer homemade but you may buy a prepared shell)
- 2 eggs
- 1 cup milk
- 1 teaspoon onion powder or two tablespoons finely shredded onions
- 1/4 teaspoon pepper
- pinch of salt, optional
- 1/4 teaspoon nutmeg, for topping

Direction

- Fry bacon in a medium frying pan until crisp (not burnt) and drain on a paper towel, set aside.
- Preheat oven to 350 degrees. In a medium bowl, combine the cheeses and sprinkle half the mixture into the pie shell. Sprinkle on the bacon bits, then cover with the remaining cheese combination. In a small bowl, combine the eggs, milk, onion powder, pepper and salt, beat until thoroughly mixed. Pour over the cheese and sprinkle with the nutmeg.
- Bake for 40-45 minutes or until firm and wooden toothpick inserted in the center comes out clean.
- Cool for 5 minutes before cutting into pie-shaped slices.

172. Quiche Lorraine With Caramelized Onions And Leeks Recipe

Serving: 6 | Prep: | Cook: 30mins | Ready in:

Ingredients

- 1 3/4 cups diced leeks, white and light green only (from about 2 large leeks,)
- 3/4 cup diced onion
- olive oil just enough to saute
- 1 1/4 cups flour
- 1 tablespoon plus 2 teaspoons cornstarch
- salt
- 6 tablespoons butter, diced
- 4 eggs, divided
- 1/2 cup plus 1 tablespoon heavy cream
- 1 cup plus 2 tablespoons sour cream
- Pinch nutmeg
- Pinch pepper
- 1 1/2 cups diced ham (1/4 -inch dice; about 1/2 pound)
- 3/4 cup grated swiss cheese

Direction

- Heat a large sauté pan over low heat.
- Sauté the leeks and onions in the olive oil 30 to 40 minutes until caramelized, occasionally stirring.
- Remove from heat and cool.
- Meanwhile, in a large bowl, combine the flour, cornstarch and one-fourth teaspoon salt.
- Cut the butter in with a pastry blender, fork or two knives until it is in very tiny bits.
- Add one egg (a fork works great for this) and mix it until a dough forms.
- (Dough can also be made in a food processor, or in in a stand mixer.)
- On a lightly floured surface, roll the dough out to a 12-inch circle.
- Place the dough in a 9-inch pie plate and press to remove any air bubbles.
- Crimp the edges, and refrigerate for 30 minutes.
- While the quiche shell chills, mix the heavy cream and sour cream in a medium bowl.
- Whisk in the remaining three eggs.
- Add a pinch each nutmeg, salt and pepper and combine to form a batter.
- Preheat the oven to 350 degrees.
- . Remove the quiche shell from the refrigerator and spread the leek and onion mixture evenly over the base.
- Sprinkle the ham and then the cheese over the leeks and onions.

- Pour in the batter and place the quiche in the oven.
- Bake until puffed and golden, about 25 to 30 minutes or puffed and golden.
- Remove from the oven and cool slightly on a rack.
- Serve warm or at room temperature.

---

173. Quiche Recipe

Serving: 12 | Prep: | Cook: 60mins | Ready in:

Ingredients

- 2 c macaroni, uncooked
- 6-8 slices bacon, chopped
- 2 c American cheese, shredded
- 2 c monterey jack cheese, shredded
- 2 c soft bread cubes
- 1 med onion, chopped fine
- 1 sm green bell pepper, chop fine
- 4 eggs, separated
- 2 c milk
- 1 t salt
- 6 – 8 drops hot sauce
- red salsa (optional)

Direction

- Preheat oven to 325 degrees.
- Prepare macaroni according to package directions; drain.
- In a medium skillet, cook bacon until crisp; drain.
- In large bowl, combine macaroni, bacon, cheeses, bread cubes, onion and green pepper.
- In a medium bowl, beat together egg yolks, milk, salt and hot sauce.
- Add to macaroni mixture; mix well.
- In a large bowl, beat egg whites until stiff.
- Fold into macaroni mixture.
- Pour into buttered 12 in quiche dish or 13x9 in baking dish.
- Place a shallow baking dish with 1 – 2 inches water on lowest rack of 325 degree oven.

- Place quiche on centre rack.
- Bake until set and knife inserted in centre comes out clean, about 1 hour.
- Let stand 5 minutes before cutting.
- Garnish as desired.
- Serve with salsa.
- Refrigerate leftover.
- Makes 10-12 servings.

---

174. Quiche Spectacular Recipe

Serving: 8 | Prep: | Cook: 60mins | Ready in:

Ingredients

- 10" spring form pan
- 1 pie crust to overlap the side of the pan
- 1 tsp dry mustard
- 4-5 c sharp shredded cheddar cheese
- 1 qt +1/2 pt heavy cream
- 6 lg eggs
- 1 - 2 cups shredded raw spinach (mainly for color) or any vegetable or meat you like. Be creative
- sea salt and fresh ground pepper

Direction

- Preheat the oven to 450 degrees
- Place the dough inside the pan and let it overhang the sides; gently massage the crust into the pan to make it even
- Sprinkle the mustard into the bottom of crust
- Add 1/2 of the cheese even in the bottom of the crust
- Add the spinach in a layer
- Generously sprinkle with the salt and pepper
- Add remaining cheese
- Whisk the cream and eggs together and slowly pour into the pan
- Run a rolling pin or jar around the top edge of the pan to remove excess dough

- Place the pan on a cookie sheet and place into the oven
- TURN OVEN DOWN TO 325 degrees
- Bake 60-70 minutes or until center still has a little jiggle to it. It will settle as it cools
- Cool for 15-20 minutes before removing the pan sides.

175. Quiche With Summer Vegetables Recipe

Serving: 4 | Prep: | Cook: 1hours | Ready in:

Ingredients

- For the pastry:
- 175g/6oz plain flour
- 60ml/2oz oil
- 60ml/2oz water
- pinch of salt
- For the filling:
- 300g/10.5oz firm silken tofu
- 250ml/8.5oz soya cream
- 2 tbsp flour
- 2 tbsp vegan butter like Vitalite
- 1/2 tsp salt
- 1/4 tsp baking powder
- pinch of turmeric for colour but not essential
- The vegetables (parboiled for about 5 minutes):
- a handful of green beans
- 6 broccoli florets cut into small pieces
- 4 tbsp garden peas or petit pois

Direction

- 1. Start by making your pastry: combine flour, oil and salt in a bowl until the flour becomes sandy.
- 2. Then add water 1 tbsp. at a time until you have added enough to form a ball.
- 3. As we've made our pastry with oil there is no real need to chill it as it won't break unlike when made with margarine.

- 4. Roll it out with a pin and place it on your baking tin (I used an 8 inch one)
- 5. Allow the sides to roll over the edge of the tin as it will shrink slightly. Blind bake it for about 20 minutes at 180C and then trim the excess pastry off.
- 6. For the filling blend the tofu, cream, margarine, flour, baking powder and salt until it's completely smooth.
- 7. Add your parboiled veg to the pastry case and pour the tofu mix over them.
- 8. Bake between 30 and 40 minutes or until the top has gone nice and brown.

176. Quiche With Swiss And Feta Cheeses Recipe

Serving: 4 | Prep: | Cook: 30mins | Ready in:

Ingredients

- 3 fresh farm eggs
- 2 cups heavy cream
- 1/2 teaspoon nutmeg
- salt
- pepper
- herbs de provence (optional)
- 1/2 medium onion, chopped
- 1 shallot, chopped
- 2 cloves garlic, minced
- 1 1/2 cup shredded swiss cheese
- 1/2 cup feta cheese, crumbled
- 1/2 stick of salted butter
- 1 pre-made refridgerated deep dish pie crust

Direction

- Preheat oven to 350 degrees.
- Melt 2 tablespoons of butter in a sauté pan.
- Add chopped onions and shallots.
- After about 3 minutes, add garlic and cook until everything is soft and fragrant.
- Remove from heat and set aside.
- Mix eggs and cream in a large bowl.

- Add nutmeg, salt and pepper to taste.
- Add herbes de provence if using.
- Add cheeses.
- Pour into pie crust.
- Dot top with butter.
- Bake for about 25-35 minutes until golden brown on top.

177.   Quiche W Stuffing Crust Recipe

Serving: 4 | Prep: | Cook: 35mins | Ready in:

Ingredients

- 1 box stuffing mix
- 1 cup diced, cooked chicken
- 1 cup shredded swiss cheese, or cheese of your chioce
- 3 eggs, beaten
- 1 can (5oz.) evaporated milk
- pepper

Direction

- Preheat oven to 400.
- Prepare stuffing as directed on box.
- Press into a 10-inch pie pan.
- Bake for 10 minutes.
- Place chicken and cheese on top of stuffing crust.
- Combine eggs, milk, and pepper.
- Pour on over chicken and cheese.
- Bake for 30-35 minutes.

178.   Quiche Greek Style Recipe

Serving: 8 | Prep: | Cook: 45mins | Ready in:

Ingredients

- 1 ¼ pounds thick Greek sheep's milk yogurt (You can use store-bought, like FAGE brand, but not the low-fat or fat-free!!!)
- 2/3 cup cornmeal
- 2/3 cup finely chopped scallions
- 2/3 cup chopped fresh dill
- 2/3 cup chopped fresh mint
- ½ tspfreshly ground white pepper, or to taste
- sea salt
- 25-30 grape leaves, fresh or frozen
- ¼ cup olive oil

Direction

- Preheat the oven to 375 degrees F.
- In a bowl, mix the yogurt with the cornmeal.
- Add the scallions, herbs, pepper, and salt, and stir well.
- Oil an oval 12 x 9-inch glass or clay ovenproof dish and line the bottom and sides with half the leaves.
- Brush with oil and pour in the yogurt mixture.
- Top with the rest of the leaves and brush with the remaining oil. Cover loosely with aluminum foil and bake for about 45 minutes, or until set and a knife inserted in the center comes out clean.
- Let the pie cool for 10 to 15 minutes before cutting to serve.
- It can also be eaten at room temperature the next day.
- Note: You can also make individual pies in ramekins.

179.   Quick Crab Quiche Recipe

Serving: 6 | Prep: | Cook: 45mins | Ready in:

Ingredients

- 1 (9 inch) deep dish pie shells
- 1 (6 1/2 ounce) can crabmeat, flaked and drained

- 1/2 cup swiss cheese, grated (cheddar does well too)
- 6 eggs
- 1 1/2 cups light cream
- 1 tablespoon instant minced onion
- 1 tablespoon dry white wine (optional)
- 1/2 teaspoon dry mustard
- 1/2 teaspoon dried tarragon leaves, crushed

Direction

- Sprinkle crabmeat and cheese into pie shell.
- Beat together remaining ingredients.
- Pour over crabmeat and cheese.
- Bake in a preheated 357 degree oven 30-35 minutes until knife inserted in center comes out clean.
- Cool 5 minutes before serving.

180. Quick Quiche Recipe

Serving: 68 | Prep: | Cook: 1mins | Ready in:

Ingredients

- 9 inch baked pie crust(make with whole wheat flour for extra special crust)
- 8 slices of bacon,cooked, crumbled , and drained
- 3 eggs, beaten
- 1 cup sour cream
- 3/4 tsp salt
- 1 tsp Worcestershire(optional)
- 1 cup swiss cheese, coarsely grated(can use1/2 Monterey Jack and 1/2 Swiss)
- 1 cup. French fried onions

Direction

- Bake pie crust as directed.
- After cooking and draining bacon, add to remaining ingredients.
- Pour into pie crust.
- Bake at 350* for 30 to 45 minutes.

181. Quick And Easy Blue Cheese Quiche Recipe

Serving: 6 | Prep: | Cook: 30mins | Ready in:

Ingredients

- 1 9-inch pie crust in aluminum tin
- 7 ounces Roquefort cheese
- 4 ounces cream cheese, room temperature
- 2/3 cup heavy cream
- 2 eggs, beaten
- Freshly grated pepper
- Pinch of cayenne pepper
- 2 tablespoons minced chives

Direction

- Preheat oven to 400 degrees.
- Prepare crust (if necessary) and set aside.
- In a large bowl, combine Roquefort cheese, cream cheese and heavy cream.
- Add the eggs, pepper, cayenne and chives and combine until well-mixed.
- Pour into the prepared pie crust and bake for 30 minutes, until the center is set.
- Remove from oven and let it rest for at least 5 minutes before serving.
- Can be served warm, at room temperature or cold.

182. Radish Leaves And Avocado Quiche Recipe

Serving: 15 | Prep: | Cook: 20mins | Ready in:

Ingredients

- 15 store-bought mini quiche shells
- 1 + 1 tablespoons of butter
- 1 shallot, finely diced
- 1 big handful of radish leaves, rinsed well, dried, chopped

- 1/2 tsp mustard
- flesh from a whole avocado, diced, mixed with a bit of lemon juice
- 1 egg
- 1 - 2 tablespoon(s) grate pecorino cheese (good match with radish)
- a dash of milk/ cream
- about 6 red radish, thinly sliced
- good pinch of salt
- grate green peppercorns
- dried juniper berries as garnish

Direction

- Pre-heat oven to 350F
- Pre-heat a skillet, sauté the shallot and butter over very low heat for about 1 minute. Raise up the heat, add radish leaves and salt for another 30 seconds. Discard any juice, set the leaves aside.
- Puree avocado and leaves, well combine with egg, cheese, mustard, milk/cream, salt and green peppers. Spoon the filling into the shells, arrange radish slices on top, dot with tiny butter cubes and a bit of salt on radish. Bake until the top slightly firm to touch, about 20 minutes.
- Garnish with juniper berries, serve warm

183.   Real Man Quiche Recipe

Serving: 8 | Prep: | Cook: 60mins | Ready in:

Ingredients

- butter flavored cooking spray
- 1 lb. sweet Italian turkey sausage links, removed from casings
- 1 medium red onion, thinly sliced
- 2 cups sliced mushrooms
- 4 cups baby spinach
- 4 eggs
- 2 egg whites
- 1/2 cup milk
- 1/4 tsp. pepper

- 6 sheets phyllo dough, defrosted according to pkg. directions
- 1/4 cup plain dry breadcrumbs
- 1/4 cup shredded gruyere cheese

Direction

- Preheat oven to 350*. Coat a 9" deep-dish glass pie pan with cooking spray.
- Cook sausage in a large non-stick skillet over medium-high heat, breaking it up into small pieces with a wooden spoon, until cooked through, about 5 minutes. Transfer to a medium bowl lined with paper towels. Coat the pan with cooking spray, add onion and mushrooms and cook, stirring until beginning to brown, 4-5 minutes. Add spinach and stir until just wilted, about 1 minute. Transfer the vegetables to the bowl with the sausage; set aside.
- In a medium bowl, whisk eggs, egg whites, milk, and pepper.
- Unroll phyllo onto a clean, dry work surface. Cover with a sheet of wax paper and then a damp kitchen towel. Place one sheet of phyllo dough into the prepared pie pan, spray with cooking spray and sprinkle lightly with breadcrumbs. Repeat with the remaining phyllo, spraying and sprinkling between each layer, turning each sheet at a 45* angle to cover the entire pan. Trim the phyllo edge with kitchen shears to be level with the rim of the pan. Spread the sausage mixture in an even layer on top of the phyllo; pour in the egg mixture and top with cheese.
- Bake the quiche until the top is browned and the phyllo is crispy, 40-45 minutes. Let cool for 10 minutes before cutting into wedges.

184.   Real Quiche Lorraine Recipe

Serving: 4 | Prep: | Cook: 15mins | Ready in:

Ingredients

- For the pastry
- 180g/6¼oz plain flour, plus extra for dusting.
- 100g/3½oz cold unsalted butter, cubed.
- 50g/2oz parmesan, grated.
- 2 tsp thyme, leaves only.
- 1 free-range egg yolk.
- 1 tsp chilled water (more if needed)
- For the filling
- 3 free-range eggs.
- 150g/5¼oz pancetta, cubed.
- 250ml/9fl oz crème fraîche.
- 150g/5¼oz Gruyère.
- freshly ground black pepper.
- Chopped curly parsley.

Direction

- Preheat the oven to 180C/350F/Gas 4. For the pastry, sieve the flour into a mixing bowl. Add the butter, parmesan and thyme and rub into the flour until the mixture resembles breadcrumbs. Add the egg yolk and the water and mix to form a firm dough. Wrap the dough in cling film and place in the fridge for 30 minutes. On a floured surface, roll out the pastry to fit one large flan tin. Line the tin with the pastry, then place a circle of baking paper over the pastry and fill with baking beans. Transfer to the oven and bake for 15 minutes. Remove the beans and paper and return to the oven for five minutes. For the filling, sauté the pancetta and shallots then place all the ingredients (except 50g/2oz of the Gruyère) into a large bowl and mix gently, to avoid filling the mixture with air. Spoon the filling into the pastry case and sprinkle the remaining Gruyère on top. Bake the quiche for 15 minutes, or until the filling is set. Serve hot or cold with a green salad.

185.   Really Delicious Ham Or Spam Quiche Recipe

Serving: 6 | Prep: | Cook: 20mins | Ready in:

Ingredients

- Spam Quiche
- 1 can Spam, cubed (small)
- *(OR) 1 cup cooked ham) *
- 1/4 cup chopped onion
- 1/4 cup chopped green pepper
- 1/8 teaspoon pepper
- 1 tablespoon cooking oil
- 2 cups milk
- 1 cup Bisquick mix
- 4 eggs
- 1 cup shredded monterey jack cheese

Direction

- Sauté Spam, onion, green pepper in oil until vegetables are tender. Spoon into lightly greased bake dish, sprinkle with cheese.
- Mix remaining ingredients in blender or with hand mixer until smooth.
- Pour evenly into pan.
- Bake at 400F for about 30 minutes.
- Let stand 5 minutes before cutting.
- ~~~~~~~~~~~~~~~~~~~~~~~~~~~~~~~~~~~~~~~
- This is a VERY nice meal with a lovely salad and fruit cup. Quite nice I thought!

186.   Reuban Quiche Recipe

Serving: 6 | Prep: | Cook: 40mins | Ready in:

Ingredients

- 1   pie crust, 9-inch unbaked
- 8 ounces corned beef - cooked and shredded
- 3/4 cup sauerkraut drained and squeezed
- 2 cups swiss cheese grated
- 2 eggs beaten
- 1 cup light cream
- 1 teaspoon onion grated
- 1/2   teaspoon dry mustard

Direction

- Preheat oven to 375F.
- Prick crust and bake for 7 minutes.
- Fill pie shell with corned beef, sauerkraut and cheese.
- Mix remaining ingredients and pour into pie shell.
- Bake 40 minutes.
- Allow to stand for 5 minutes before cutting.

187. Rice Quiche Recipe

Serving: 12 | Prep: | Cook: 50mins | Ready in:

Ingredients

- 2 cups cooked rice
- 1 pound cooked & crumbled italian sausage
- 3/4 stick of pepperoni (cut into small cubes)
- 1 large block of mozzerella cheese (cut into small cubes)
- 5-6 eggs well beaten
- 1 cup parmesan cheese
- salt & pepper
- 1/2 to 1 cup well drained roasted peppers cut into pieces

Direction

- Mix all ingredients until well blended
- Put into a greased 9 x 13 pan
- Bake 45-50 minutes or till golden brown
- Cut into squares and serve
- Optional: add olives, scallions, and mushrooms, be creative

188. Rice Crust Spinach Quiche Recipe

Serving: 8 | Prep: | Cook: 35mins | Ready in:

Ingredients

- 1-1/2c cooked brown rice
- 1c shredded swiss cheese divided
- 1/4 tsp curry powder
- 3/4 c egg subsitute
- 1 pkg frozen spinach thawed and squeezed
- 3/4 c evaporated skim milk
- 1 small can mushrooms or 1/2 c fresh
- 2 T chopped onion
- 1/4 tsp garlic powder
- 1/8-1/4 tsp pepper

Direction

- Combine rice, 1/2c cheese, 1/4 c egg substitute and curry powder.
- Press into a 9in pie plate.
- Microwave 5 minutes or until firm.
- Combine Spinach, milk, mushrooms, cheese, egg substitute, onion, and seasonings.
- Microwave 50% for 20 minutes.
- Cool 5 minutes.
- When figured it came to 2.6 plus points so I rounded it to 3.

189. Salmon Broccoli Quiche With Rice Crust Recipe

Serving: 6 | Prep: | Cook: 50mins | Ready in:

Ingredients

- 1 3/4 cups packed cooked rice
- 1 cup egg whites
- 3/4 plain low-fat yogurt
- 2 tbsp, parsley, broken in Dijon mustard
- 1/4 tsp salt (for no-salt recipe, use 1 tsp McCormick's 'no-salt-added Citrus & pepper)
- 1 can red salmon (or tuna) drained, broken into chunks
- 1 cup finely chopped broccoli
- 1/3 cup finely chopped red onion

Direction

- Mix rice with 3 tbsp. of the eggs.

- Press the mixture over the sides and bottom of greased 9 inch pie plate.
- Bake @ 235*F for 10 minutes.
- Whisk remaining egg with yogurt, mustard, parsley and salt (or salt substitute).
- Place salmon in the rice crust with broccoli and onion.
- Pour egg mixture over all.
- Bake 35 to 40 minutes, or until set.
- Variations:
- Sprinkle with 1/2 cup shredded cheddar cheese or Tex Mex before baking; or --- instead of salmon or tuna, substitute with 1 cup coarsely chopped crab meat.

190. Salmon Quiche Recipe

Serving: 6 | Prep: | Cook: 45mins | Ready in:

Ingredients

- For the Pastry....
- 125gm margarine
- 1/2 cup plain flour
- 1/4 tsp salt
- 1/2 cup self raising flour
- 1 egg, beaten
- 1/4 cup water (approx)
- For the FIlling.....
- 220gm can flaked salmon
- 1/2 cup chopped shallots, green tops included
- 1 sliced tomato
- 1 cup milk
- 1 cup grated cheese
- 3 eggs
- 1 cup cream

Direction

- For the Pastry
- Sift flour and salt into a bowl and rub in margarine until mixture resembles bread crumbs.

- Mix egg with water and stir into flour - work into a firm dough, adding more water if necessary.
- Roll onto a floured board and line a 24cm quiche dish.
- Place in refrigerator for one hour.
- For the Filling
- Spread the flaked salmon, grated cheese and shallots over the chilled pastry base.
- Beat eggs, add milk, cream, salt and pepper and gently pour over filling.
- Place sliced tomato evenly on top and bake approximately 45 mins in a 160°C oven.
- Serving Suggestion
- Serve with a tossed salad.
- Leftover Potential
- Can be eaten cold, or reheated easily for a tasty snack.

191. Salmon And Swiss Cheese Quiche Recipe

Serving: 6 | Prep: | Cook: 40mins | Ready in:

Ingredients

- 1 9-inch pastry shell, unbaked
- ¾ cup onion, finely chopped
- ¼ cup green pepper, coarsely chopped
- 2 tablespoons butter or margarine
- 2 cups swiss cheese, cubed
- 1 7 ounce can salmon, drained and flaked
- 1 tablespoon lemon juice
- 1 8-ounce container sour cream
- 3 eggs
- 1 tablespoon all-purpose flour
- 2 teaspoons instant chicken bouillon powder
- bread crumbs, buttered

Direction

- Preheat oven to 450 degrees.
- Bake pie shell for 8 minutes, remove from oven.

- Reduce temperature to 350 degrees.
- Cook onion and pepper in butter until tender.
- Arrange cheese in bottom of pastry shell.
- Toss salmon with lemon juice, arrange over cheese.
- Beat together sour cream, eggs, cooked onions and pepper, flour and bouillon powder.
- Pour over salmon.
- Top with buttered bread crumbs.
- Bake approximately 30 minutes or until golden brown and knife inserted in center comes out clean.
- Let stand 10 minutes.

192.   Sausage Onion Quiche Recipe

Serving: 6 | Prep: | Cook: 30mins |Ready in:

Ingredients

- 1 pound pork sausage (we prefer one of the spicy/zesty ones)
- 1 medium onion, chopped
- 1/2 cup finely diced celery
- 1 1/2 cups shredded cheddar cheese
- 3 eggs, beaten
- 1 cup half-and-half
- 2 tablespoons flour
- 1/2 teaspoon salt
- 1/2 teaspoon paprika
- unbaked 9 inch pie shell

Direction

- Partially cook sausage. Remove from pan and keep 2 tablespoons of rendered fat in the pan for the next step.
- Sauté onion and celery in the reserved fat for 2-3 minutes.
- Put with sausage and cheese into the pie shell.
- Mix remaining ingredients and pour into the shell.

- Bake in 400 degree oven for 30 minutes or until browned and filling is just set.
- Cool 10 minutes and serve.

193.   Sausage Spinach Quiche Recipe

Serving: 6 | Prep: | Cook: 45mins |Ready in:

Ingredients

- 1- pastry pie shell...............or make your own........ i like the refrigerated ones when im in a hurry...........
- 8 -ounces bulk pork sausage :.... i use the hot sausage !! i like the spice
- 1/4 -cup chopped onion
- 1 -clove garlic, minced
- 1 -10-ounce package frozen chopped spinach
- 1- to 1 1/2 -cup shredded cheddar cheese (4 ounces) .... i use 1/2 cheddar and 1/2 pepperjack cheese........ and i always put extra cheese lol...............use what you like..........
- 4- eggs, slightly beaten
- 1- cup light cream
- 1/4- teaspoon salt
- 3- cherry tomatoes, halved (optional)
- watercress sprigs (optional)

Direction

- Prepare pastry and set aside.
- Crumble sausage in medium skillet; add onion and garlic.
- Cook over medium heat till sausage is browned, stirring occasionally; drain well.
- Thaw spinach, drain well.
- Remove remaining moisture by pressing spinach between layers of paper towel.
- Add spinach to sausage mixture; mix well.
- Sprinkle cheese evenly in pastry shell.
- Top with sausage mixture. In a medium mixing bowl combine eggs, cream and salt; mix well.
- Pour egg mixture over sausage mixture.

- Bake in a 375 degree F. oven for 45 minutes or until a knife inserted halfway between center and outer edge comes out clean.
- Let stand 10 minutes before serving.
- Garnish with cherry tomatoes and watercress, if desired.
- Serves 6

194. Seafood Cream Cheese Quiche Recipe

Serving: 6 | Prep: | Cook: 40mins | Ready in:

Ingredients

- 1- 8" unbaked pie shell
- stalk of celery, chopped
- 1/2 small onion, chopped
- 8 ounces cream cheese
- 1/4 lb. Grated swiss cheese
- 1 lb. shrimp, shelled and deveined
- 3 Tbs. melted butter
- 5 large eggs
- 1 cup milk

Direction

- Ingredients make two 8" pies.
- Preheat oven to 425 degrees.
- Melt butter in pan and sauté shrimp, onion and celery.
- Cut cream cheese into 1/4 inch pieces. Cover the bottom of the pie crust with the cream cheese pieces.
- Add the sautéed shrimp, onion and celery and top with the grated Swiss cheese.
- Mix together the milk and eggs and pour over the top.
- Bake 10 minutes, then reduce temperature to 350 and bake for another 1/2 hour.

195. Shamrock Spinach Quiche Recipe

Serving: 8 | Prep: | Cook: 45mins | Ready in:

Ingredients

- * 10 oz frozen chopped spinach
- * 4 serving Louis Rich, turkey bacon
- * 2 tbsp 50/50 butter Blend With extra virgin olive oil
- * 1 cup Finely Shredded swiss cheese
- * 1/2 cup onions, Chopped
- * 1 stlk celery, raw, diced
- * 1/2 cup Raw Shredded carrots
- * 2 cloves garlic Clove
- * 1 tsp ground thyme
- * 1/2 tsp cayenne pepper
- * 1 pie crust Pillsbury pie crusts
- * 1 cup Fat -free cottage cheese
- * 1 tsp nutmeg, Ground
- * 1/2 cup egg Beaters
- * 1 cup Fat Free milk

Direction

- Pre-bake the pie shell until partially done as instructed on carton.
- Wrap the bacon in paper towels and cook in microwave on high for 90 seconds. Let drain, cool then dice.
- Sauté the onion, carrot, garlic and celery in butter until the onion is soft. When the veggies are looking soft and lovely, add the thawed/drained spinach to the pan and mix well. Cook just a bit longer to make sure any extra liquid is cooked off.
- Spread cottage cheese over the bottom of the pastry shell.
- Mix the spinach with the bacon, onion/celery mixture and spread over top of the cottage cheese.
- Sprinkle Swiss cheese over top.
- Combine the eggs, milk, spices and pour over all.
- Bake at 350°F (175°C) 45 minutes.

196. Silentwriters Spinach Quiche Recipe

Serving: 6 | Prep: | Cook: 47mins | Ready in:

Ingredients

- 1-frozen pie shell
- 4-eggs lightly beaten
- 1 cup of milk (any kind)
- 1-package (10-16) ozs chopped frozen spinach, thawed and squeezed dry.
- 1 cup chopped onions (or) small onion
- salt & pepper To taste
- 2/3 cup (or less) of shredded cheddar cheese
- 2/3 cup (or less) of smoked swiss cheese (or regular)
- 2/3 cup (or less) of provolone cheese
- 1 Whole garlic (or) garlic Poweder to taste

Direction

- Preheat oven to 350 degrees F.
- Beat eggs until well blended.
- Add milk.
- Sauté onions & garlic in saucepan for about 7 minutes.
- DO NOT BROWN.
- Add Spinach to saucepan with eggs & milk blend.
- Add cheeses to same pot mix together.
- DO NOT COOK IN PAN.
- Add this mixture to the pie shell.
- Bake in oven at 350 deg. for 40-45 mins.
- Remove from oven and allow to sit until slightly cooled.
- Eat either warm or refrigerate and eat cold.

197. Simple Crust Less Skillet Quiche Recipe

Serving: 4 | Prep: | Cook: 1hours | Ready in:

Ingredients

- Ingredients:
- • 6 large eggs, beaten.
- • 1 cup frozen mixed vegetables, or make up your own mix.
- • 1 cup (4 oz.) grated Swiss or cheddar cheese. Cheese of choice and up to ½ cup, depending on if your choice is firm or soft.
- • 1 cup Half and Half or light cream.
- • 2 Tbs. butter.
- • 1 Tbs. minced onion.
- • 1 medium bell pepper, seeded and course chopped.
- • ½ tsp. salt, to taste.
- • ½-1 tsp. dried marjoram or oregano leaves, crushed.
- • 1 cup of sliced mushrooms or a hand full of Enoki mushrooms, cut once or twice.
- • 1 medium clove of garlic, fine minced, to taste.
- • 1/8 tsp. pepper, to taste.
- • Fresh dill (optional).

Direction

- 1. Beat together all ingredients except mushrooms, butter and dill until well blended.
- 2. In 10 inch skillet, over very low heat, melt butter.
- 3. Pour in egg mixture and distribute ingredients evenly.
- 4. Cook, covered, without stirring over low heat until eggs are almost set, about 15-18 minutes.
- 5. Remove from heat, sprinkle the sliced or Enoki mushrooms over the top, cover and let stand until knife inserted in center comes out clean, 10 to 15 minutes. I cover the skillet lid with a folded dish towel to keep in the heat and set the quiche.
- 6. To serve, cut in wedges or, if you must, spoon out of pan.
- 7. Garnish with fresh dill if desired.
- A nice mixed green salad and some crusty bread go well. We're trying to ease up on the

gluten a bit so I did a mix of ½ wild rice and ½ white rice this time.

---

198. Simple Meaty Quiche Recipe

Serving: 16 | Prep: | Cook: 75mins |Ready in:

Ingredients

- 2 deep dish pie shells
- 1 dozen eggs
- 1 pkg breakfast sausage (NOT spicy variety)
- 1 pkg "Ready to Serve" bacon (15 slices)
- -may use regular raw bacon, cooked but remember this is a
- SIMPLE recipe
- 16 oz diced cooked ham (i buy the chunky salad kind when i can
- but usually dice up the cheap lunchmeant ham)
- 16 oz pkg grated cheddar/monterray jack

Direction

- Preheat oven to 425 degrees. Remove pie shells from package and, using a fork, poke several holes at the bottom of the pie shells. The pie shells will bake for 10 minutes; set aside, and change the oven temperature to 375 degrees.
- Begin browning the breakfast sausage (as you would ground beef).
- While the sausage is browning you may begin microwaving the bacon and setting it aside on a plate with paper towels. When the sausage is done browning, drain and set aside.
- Dice the ham (if you need to) into approximately 1/2 inch squares.
- Chop the bacon into small 1/2 inch pieces as well.
- Layer all ingredients into both pie shells.
- Beat the entire dozen eggs (or 6 at a time if you prefer) and pour equal amount over each pie.

- Sprinkle all cheese on top of pies covering all the egg.
- Bake for 60 minutes and check quiches by inserting fork into center. If it's extremely juicy it will need to cook for another 15 minutes. Let sit 10 minutes before serving. (It's the perfect time to throw together a colorful salad!)

---

199. Simple Quiche 2 Recipe

Serving: 6 | Prep: | Cook: 40mins |Ready in:

Ingredients

- 1 tsp. unsalted butter
- 1/2 tsp salt to taste - remember ham can be salty
- 1/2 cup onion, chopped
- 1/4 lb. sliced cooked ham, chopped
- 1/2 lb. fat-free swiss cheese, shredded
- 2 Tbs. all purpose flour
- 3 eggs, beaten
- 1 cup buttermilk
- 1/8 tsp. ground nutmeg
- 1 frozen 9 inch pie shell

Direction

- Preheat oven to 400°F.
- Melt butter in a heavy non-stick skillet over medium high heat.
- Sauté onion 5 minutes, or until tender.
- Transfer onion and next 3 ingredients to a bowl.
- Combine eggs and buttermilk in another bowl.
- Season with salt to taste and stir in onion mixture.
- Pour into pie shell.
- Sprinkle nutmeg on top.
- Bake 35-45 minutes or until center is set.

200.   Simple Quiche Recipe

Serving: 8 | Prep: | Cook: 60mins | Ready in:

Ingredients

- 2 deep dish pie shells
- 1 dozen eggs
- 1 pkg breakfast sausage
- 1 pkg "Ready to Serve" bacon (15 slices) (regular bacon is ok to use-   but messier and i go for the simpler the better)
- 16 oz cubed, cooked ham (I buy the cubed salad ham when i can but
- I usually use the cheap ham lunchmeat and cube it)
- 16 oz pkg shredded cheddar/monteray jack mixed

Direction

- Preheat oven to 425 degrees. Remove pie shells from package and poke holes in bottom of crusts with a fork. Bake for 10 minutes and set aside. Change oven temperature to 375 degrees.
- Brown breakfast sausage as you would ground beef and drain.
- Microwave bacon and let drain on a plate with paper towels. Dice once it's cooled a bit.
- Cube ham into about 1/2 inch pieces (if you're using the lunchmeat)
- Layer all meats into each pie crusts.
- Beat the entire dozen eggs (or 6 at a time if you prefer) and pour over each pie.
- Sprinkle cheese over each pie covering all the filling.
- Bake for 60 minutes. Insert fork into center and if quiche is still extremely juicy let it cook 15 more minutes. Remove from oven and let cool for 10 minutes before serving. (Perfect time to make that colorful salad!)

201.   Simply Quiche Lorraine Recipe

Serving: 6 | Prep: | Cook: 45mins | Ready in:

Ingredients

- 1 nine inch prepared pie crust.
- 12 slices of bacon fried crisp, drained and crumbled.
- 1 cup shredded swiss cheese.
- 1/3 cup finely chopped onion.
- 4 eggs
- 2 cups half and half
- 3/4 tsp salt
- 1/4 tsp pepper
- 1/8 tsp cayenne pepper (optional)

Direction

- OK, so I cheat a little here and there. I use a store bought piecrust. I was never good at those.
- Fry the bacon up crisp, remove from skillet, drain on paper towel.
- Beat the eggs slightly in a small bowl.
- Whisk in the remaining ingredients except the chopped onion.
- Line the bottom of the piecrust with the crumbled bacon.
- Layer the chopped onion on top of the bacon.
- Then add a layer of shredded cheese.
- Pour the egg mixture over the top of the other ingredients.
- Preheat the oven to 425 degrees F. Cover the edge of the piecrust with foil.
- Place the pie in the oven and cook uncovered for 15 minutes.
- Reduce the oven temperature to 300 degrees F. Continue to bake for about 30 minutes or until a knife inserted half way between the edge and the center comes out clean.
- Let stand for 10 minutes, cut and serve hot.

202. Smoked Salmon Quiche Recipe

Serving: 25 | Prep: | Cook: 50mins | Ready in:

Ingredients

- 1/2 cup crushed round crackers
- 8 oz. smoked salmon
- 2 (8-ounce) packages cream cheese, softened
- 4 eggs
- 1 cup monterey jack cheese, shredded
- 1/2 cup sour cream
- 2 tsp. Dijon mustard
- 1/4 cup red onion, minced
- 1/4 cup red bell pepper, chopped
- 1/4 cup green bell pepper, chopped
- 1 teaspoon dried dillweed
- 1/4 teaspoon cayenne pepper

Direction

- Sprinkle cracker crumbs in bottom of a lightly greased 9-inch springform pan; set aside.
- Beat cream cheese at medium speed of electric mixer until fluffy. Add eggs, one at a time, beating well after each addition. Add remaining ingredients and mix until well blended. Pour into prepared pan. Bake at 325 degrees F. for 45 to 50 minutes. Cool on a wire rack for 10 minutes. Gently run a knife around edge of pan; release sides of pan. Cool completely. Refrigerate until serving time. Serve at room temperature with crackers.

203. Smoked Sausage And Potato Mini Quiche Recipe

Serving: 12 | Prep: | Cook: 35mins | Ready in:

Ingredients

- 1 bag frozen hashbrowns, thawed and squeezed dry (30 oz)
- 1/4 cup butter, melted

- 4 large eggs, lightly beaten
- 1 cup half and half
- 1 teaspoon dry mustard
- 1 teaspoon salt
- 1/2 teaspoon ground black pepper
- 1 cup finely chopped smoked sausage
- 1 cup finely shredded sharp cheddar cheese
- garnish: fresh parsley

Direction

- Preheat oven to 425 degrees; spray two 12 cup muffin pans with cooking spray.
- Press hash browns into bottom and up sides of muffin cups.
- Gently brush with melted butter.
- Bake crusts 20 minutes; reduce heat to 350 degrees.
- In a medium bowl, whisk together eggs, half and half, dry mustard, salt and pepper until well combined.
- Evenly divide sausage and cheese between crusts.
- Spoon egg mixture into each crust.
- Bake 15 minutes; cool in pans 5 minutes before removing.
- Garnish with parsley, if desired.

204. Southwestern Quiche Recipe

Serving: 8 | Prep: | Cook: 30mins | Ready in:

Ingredients

- 1 unbaked 9" pie shell
- 4 eggs
- 1 teaspoon salt
- 1/2 cup chopped onion
- 1 teaspoon red chile powder
- 1 teaspoon black pepper
- 1 cup chopped green chile
- 2 cups heavy cream or 1 cup evaporated milk or 1 cup half & half

- 1 cup shredded swiss cheese
- 1/2 cup crumbled cooked bacon

Direction

- Separate eggs and beat egg yolks.
- Whip egg whites until thick and foamy.
- Fold egg whites into yokes along with salt, onions, red chili powder, black pepper and green chili.
- Add cream or evaporated milk to mixture and blend well.
- Layer Swiss cheese over bottom of pie crust and then pour egg mixture into pie crust.
- Sprinkle crumbled bacon over top.
- Bake at 425 degrees for 25-30 minutes or until browned and solid.
- Serve hot.

---

205.   Southwestern Quiche With Potato Crust Recipe

Serving: 6 | Prep: | Cook: 15mins | Ready in:

Ingredients

- 6 large eggs
- 1 tsp. salt
- 1.5 cups frozen shredded hash brown potatoes, thawed
- 1/2 medium red bell pepper, diced
- 1/2 cup fresh or frozen corn kernels, thawed if frozen
- 2 green onions (white and green parts), thinly sliced
- 2 tbsp. chopped fresh cilantro
- 3/4 cup shredded or crumbled cheddar cheese
- 1/2 cup low-fat milk
- 2 chipotle chiles in adobo sauce, w/ 2 tsp. sauce reserved

Direction

- Preheat oven to 375 degrees F. Coat the pie dish with cooking spray. Whisk together 1 egg and 1/4 tsp. salt in a medium bowl. Stir in shredded hash browns. Press the potato mixture into the bottom and sides of the pie dish to form crust. Bake for 15 minutes, or until lightly browned.
- Sprinkle the bell pepper, corn, green onions, cilantro, and cheese over the potato crust.
- In a blender, mix together the remaining eggs, milk, 3/4 tsp. salt, chilies and adobo sauce. Pour mixture over vegetables in pie dish. Bake 20 to 25 minutes, or until knife inserted in center comes out clean. Let stand 5 minutes before serving.
- Serves 6.
- I served the quiche topped with avocado slices and good store-bought salsa (I had Mrs. Renfro's Black Bean Salsa on hand). It was quite tasty, and everyone wanted seconds. I'll make this again, but I think next time I'll serve it with some black beans or a salad on the side, to add some fiber, and maybe add a third chipotle pepper (love the smoky flavor they add). Adapted from January 2007 Vegetarian Times recipe.

---

206.   Spinach And Chicken Quiche Recipe

Serving: 4 | Prep: | Cook: 1hours | Ready in:

Ingredients

- 1 cup (4 ounces) shredded cheddar cheese, divided
- 1 unbaked pastry shell (9 inches)
- 1 cup diced cooked chicken
- 1 package (10 ounces) frozen chopped spinach, thawed and squeezed dry
- 1/4 cup finely chopped onion
- 2 eggs
- 3/4 cup milk
- 3/4 cup mayonnaise
- 1/4 teaspoon salt
- 1/8 teaspoon pepper

Direction

- Sprinkle 1/4 cup cheese into the pastry shell. In a large bowl, combine the chicken, 1/2 cup spinach, onion and remaining cheese (save remaining spinach for another use). Spoon into pastry shell. In a small bowl, whisk the eggs, milk, mayonnaise, salt and pepper; pour over the chicken mixture.
- Bake at 350° for 40-45 minutes or until a knife inserted near the center comes out clean. Let stand for 15 minutes before cutting.

207.　　Spinach And Ham Pie Quiche Recipe

Serving: 46 | Prep: | Cook: 110mins | Ready in:

Ingredients

- 1 8 oz package cream cheese, softened
- 4 eggs
- 1 cup evaporated milk
- 1/4 tsp. ground red pepper (or to taste)
- 1/2 tsp. seasoning salt
- 1 pkg. (10 oz) frozen, chopped spinach, thawed and squeezed dry
- 1 cup diced ham
- 1/2 cup finely chopped onion
- 1 prepared, deep dish pie crust, thawed

Direction

- Preheat oven to 350.
- In a medium mixing bowl, beat cream cheese until fluffy. Beat in eggs, milk, and seasonings. Should be well mixed and uniform when finished beating.
- Stir in the spinach, ham and onion with large spoon.
- Pour into prepared deep dish crust.
- Bake at 350 for one hour, or until knife inserted near middle comes out clean

---

208.　　Spinach And Muenster Quiche Bites Recipe

Serving: 32 | Prep: | Cook: 30mins | Ready in:

Ingredients

- 1 10oz package frozen chopped spinach
- 2 T olive oil
- 1 c sliced fresh mushrooms
- 1/2 c chopped onion
- 1/2 c chopped red pepper
- 6 large eggs
- 1/4 t ground white pepper
- /14 t nutmeg
- 1/4 t salt
- 2 8-oz ;ackages muenster cheese, grated

Direction

- Preheat oven to 350
- In large skillet, heat oil over med heat
- Add mushrooms, onions, red pepper, spinach, and seasonings
- Cook until veggies are soft
- Drain in paper towel lined colander
- Whisk eggs in large bowl
- Stir in spinach mixture
- Add cheese
- Pour into lightly greased 9x13 baking dish
- Bake 25-20 minutes or until lightly browned
- Cool for 10 minutes
- Cut into squares and serve
- ** Great with fresh fruit as a side

209.　　Spinach Feta Quiche Recipe

Serving: 6 | Prep: | Cook: 60mins | Ready in:

Ingredients

- For the crust:

- 1 1/2 cups all-purpose flour
- 1/2 tsp salt
- 1/2 cup cold butter (you can use shortening if you like, but remember, butter makes it better, or so I say)
- 3-6 Tablespoons ice water (the range is big, I know, but I find sometimes I need more and sometimes I need less.
- For the spinach and feta Filling:
- One box of frozen chopped leaf spinach (if you want to go to your friendly local organic farmer-emphasis on local- and use fresh spinach from them, by all means do so. If I had been making on Sunday, I may have been using some from the farmer's market).
- 1 medium yellow onion, diced.
- 2 or 3 cloves of garlic, minced or pressed.
- 2 Tbsps butter (the amount of butter and olive oil can be cut down if you prefer)
- 2 Tbsps olive oil
- 8 ounces feta cheese
- 3 eggs
- 2 egg yolks
- 1 cup heavy cream or whole milk
- nutmeg to taste
- salt and pepper to taste

Direction

- For the Crust:
- -Mix the flour and the salt together in a medium bowl.
- -Cut the butter into the flour and salt mixture until it resembles coarse peas (I did use pastry cutter for this today, as my hands seemed a bit hot, but by all means, get your hands into the dough!)
- -Drizzle the ice water over the top of the dough (I start with 3 Tbsps. and add more if needed) and gently mix the dough until it starts to come together. Form the shaggy dough into a disk and send it off to the refrigerator for about a half hour rest before rolling.
- For the Spinach and Feta Filling and Quiche Assembly:
- -Preheat the oven to 375 degrees f.

- -Thaw and drain the spinach until it is as dry as you can get it. You may want to chop it up a bit more.
- -Heat the olive oil and butter over medium heat until the butter is melted and bubbly.
- -Sweat the onion and garlic in the olive oil mixture until the onions are translucent (enjoy the wonderful smell of cooking garlic and onion while doing this. Yum).
- -Add the spinach to this mixture and continue cooking until the spinach is heated through. Remove from the heat.
- -Crumble the feta into the spinach mixture and mix together. Set aside to cool.
- -Pull your pie dough out of the refrigerator and roll out on a lightly floured board to the size you need for your pie tin (I used a 9" pie tin, somewhat shallow).
- -Place the rolled out dough in the tin, place the spinach mixture in the dough.
- -Beat together the eggs, yolks and cream. Add a little grate of nutmeg, fresh ground pepper and a pinch of salt (you won't need too much salt, as the feta is rather salty). Pour this mixture over the spinach/feta mix in the pie shell and mix together with your hands (or a spoon if you would rather not get your hands into this) carefully so as not to puncture the crust.
- -Flute or fold the edges of your pie crust (I like to just fold over the excess crust for a rustic look). You can either bake this now, or chill until you need it.
- -Bake for about 45-60 minutes, or until a lovely brown on top and the eggs have set up.
- -Serve hot with a salad, serve cold with a salad, and serve however you like!

210.   Spinach Gouda And Mushroom Quiche Recipe

Serving: 6 | Prep: | Cook: 45mins | Ready in:

Ingredients

- 1 recipe Pastry shell for single crust pie
- 1/2 up Chopped onion
- 1 tbsp butter
- 8 eggs
- 1 1/2 cup mushrooms
- 1/2 cup sour cream
- 1/2 cup half-and-half, light cream or milk
- 1/4 tsp salt
- 1/8 tsp pepper
- 3 cups fresh spinach, snipped
- 1 1/4 cups Shredded smoked gouda cheese

Direction

- Bake crust at 425 in an 8 inch pie or tart pan until set and dry. (8-12 minutes)
- Sauté onions in butter until transparent
- In a medium bowl, beat eggs lightly with a fork.
- Stir in sour cream and light cream, salt and pepper.
- Stir in onion, spinach, and cheese
- Pour egg mixture into the hot, baked pastry crust.
- Bake at 325 degrees for about 45 minutes, or until a knife inserted into the center comes out clean.
- Let quiche rest for 10 minutes before serving.

211. Spinach Mozzarella Quiche Recipe

Serving: 0 | Prep: | Cook: 1hours30mins |Ready in:

Ingredients

- 6 large eggs
- 1 cup whole milk
- 1 cup mozzarella cheese, shredded
- 1 cup frozen chopped spinach, thawed and drained
- 1 medium onion, diced
- 3 cloves garlic, minced
- 1 teaspoon salt

- 1/2 teaspoon black pepper, ground
- 1 unbaked pie crust

Direction

- Preheat oven to 350 degrees.
- Place the pie crust in a pie dish and set aside.
- In a medium pan, sauté the onion and garlic till caramelized.
- In a medium bowl blend eggs and milk till evenly mixed.
- Add the spinach, onion and garlic to the egg and milk mixture.
- Next add the cheese and mix well till evenly incorporated.
- Pour the mixture into the unbaked pie crust.
- Sprinkle the top with a little more mozzarella if desired.
- Place pie in oven and cook till golden and puffed up in the center.
- It should be done in no more than an hour.
- When done the quiche should sit for about 5 minutes before serving.
- Serve warm.
- Refrigerate leftovers.

212. Spinach Quiche With Feta Cheese Recipe

Serving: 6 | Prep: | Cook: 40mins |Ready in:

Ingredients

- 10 Oz frozen chopped spinach
- 4 eggs Well Beaten
- 3/4 Cup Cream
- 1 1/4 Cup milk
- 2 tb lemon juice
- 2 tb parsley, chopped
- 1/4 lb feta cheese, crumbled
- 3 tb Parmesan or romano cheese

Direction

- Start with a lightly baked and cooled pie shell

- Defrost spinach and squeeze out as much moisture as possible; it should be fairly dry.
- Mix the eggs, cream, and milk.
- Add the salt and pepper, lemon juice, and parsley.
- Stir in the spinach and feta cheese.
- Fill the quiche crust, and place the Parmesan on top.
- Bake at 375 F. for 30 to 40 minutes, or until a knife inserted in the center comes out dry.
- Cool for 10 minutes before serving.
- Can also be served at room temperature.

213. Spinach Quiche The Best Ever Recipe

Serving: 8 | Prep: | Cook: 70mins | Ready in:

Ingredients

- 1 deep dish pie crust
- 1/2 bag spinach, chopped
- 1 cup zucchini, grated
- 1/3 cup feta cheese
- 1/2 cup onion, chopped
- 1 teaspoon crushed garlic
- 1/4 cup grated parmesan cheese
- 1/2 cup mozzarella cheese
- 1/2 cup plain yogurt
- 1/2 cup cream
- 4 eggs
- 1 tablespoon flour
- 1 teaspoon salt
- 1/4 teaspoon oregano
- 1/4 teaspoon nutmeg

Direction

- Preheat oven to 425 degrees.
- Mix together all ingredients except pie crust (obviously)
- Bake pie crust for 7 minutes
- Reduce heat to 325
- Pour filling into crust

- Bake 1 hour or until knife inserted in center comes out clean
- Let cool and enjoy!

214. Spinach Red Pepper And Feta Quiche Recipe

Serving: 4 | Prep: | Cook: 55mins | Ready in:

Ingredients

- 1 frozen prepared deep dish pie shell
- 3 tablespoons extra-virgin olive oil
- 1 cup chopped onion
- 1 large red pepper finely chopped
- 3 garlic cloves, minced
- 12oz. fresh baby spinach, briefly chopped
- 3 large eggs
- 1/4 cup grated Parmesan
- 1 cup milk
- 2/3 cup (3 ounces) crumbled feta

Direction

- Preheat oven to 350 degrees F.
- Blind bake the crust: Line the pie shell with aluminum foil and weight it with pie weights or beans. Bake for 15 to 20 minutes until light golden brown.
- Increase oven temperature to 375 degrees F.
- In a large skillet, heat oil over moderate heat. Add onion along with red pepper and cook until softened. Turn up heat to moderately high. Add garlic and spinach and cook, stirring until just heated through. Drain off any excess liquid. Beat the eggs in a bowl and add the Parmesan and milk. Add the spinach mixture and feta, and pour into the pie shell. Bake on a sheet pan in the middle of the oven for 50 to 55 minutes or until just set.
- Note: Be sure the spinach mix is as dray as possible before adding to bowl.

215.   Spinach And Bacon Quiche Recipe

Serving: 8 | Prep: | Cook: 40mins | Ready in:

Ingredients

- 6 large eggs beaten
- 1-1/2 cups heavy cream
- 1/2 teaspoon salt
- 1 teaspoon freshly ground black pepper
- 2 cups chopped fresh baby spinach packed
- 1 pound bacon cooked and crumbled
- 1-1/2 cups shredded swiss cheese
- 1 refrigerated 9" pie crust fitted to a glass pie plate

Direction

- Preheat oven to 375.
- Combine eggs, cream, salt and pepper in a blender.
- Layer spinach, bacon and cheese in the bottom of the pie crust.
- Pour egg mixture on top.
- Bake 40 minutes until egg mixture is set then cut into 8 wedges.

216.   Spinach And Cream Cheese Quiche Recipe

Serving: 10 | Prep: | Cook: 60mins | Ready in:

Ingredients

- Pastry
- 150ml self-raising flour
- 75g butter, cut into small cubes
- 1 tsp salt
- Cold water to mix
- Filling
- 230g Lancewood Plain cream cheese
- 900g fresh spinach, washed thoroughly to remove all grit. Discard stalks and damaged leaves
- 25g butter
- 150ml milk
- 4 eggs, beaten
- 2 Tbls parmesan cheese - grated
- Freshly grated nutmeg
- 1 tsp freshly squeezed lemon juice
- salt and freshly ground black pepper

Direction

- Pre-heat oven to 180 C.
- Pastry:
- Sift the flour and salt into a large mixing bowl.
- Add butter and Transfer to a food processor and process till mixture resembles breadcrumbs.
- With the processor running, add the water little by little till a soft dough forms.
- Remove to a floured surface, roll into a ball.
- Cover with cling film and place in refrigerator to chill for 20 minutes, before rolling out.
- Line a 25-cm quiche tin with pastry and prick base all over with a fork.
- Bake for 15 minutes.
- Remove from oven, brush pastry case with beaten egg and bake for a further 5 minutes.
- Remove from oven and set aside.
- Filling:
- Drain spinach leaves thoroughly. Place them in a saucepan together with the butter and some salt and pepper. Cover and cook for about 7 minutes, stirring occasionally until the spinach is limp but colour is still bright.
- Drain thoroughly, pressing out excess liquid.
- Beat Cream Cheese in a bowl and gradually add the milk, beaten eggs, parmesan cheese and the seasoning.
- Chop up drained spinach and stir into cream mixture, adding lemon juice and more seasoning if needed.
- Pour mixture into pastry casing and bake for 35 minutes or until filling is firm and golden in colour.

217. Springtime If It Ever Gets Here Quiche Recipe

Serving: 6 | Prep: | Cook: 45mins | Ready in:

Ingredients

- CRUST....Buy one.
- FILLING
- 2 cups shredded sharp cheddar cheese
- 1 cup shredded cooked chicken
- 6 slices crisply cooked bacon, crumbled
- 1/4 lb. fresh asparagus
- 1&1/2 cups half&half
- 2 Tbs. chopped chives
- 4 eggs slightly beaten
- 1/4 tsp. sea salt
- 1/8 tsp. pepper

Direction

- Pre-heat oven to 400.
- Spread cheese over bottom of crust and top with chicken.
- Sprinkle bacon over chicken.
- Place asparagus spears in spoke pattern on top of bacon.
- In a small bowl mix eggs, chives, half &half, salt and pepper.
- Pour over chicken mixture in pie crust.
- Bake for 40 to 45 minutes until golden and set in the middle.
- Let stand 10 minutes and serve.

218. Summer Quiche Recipe

Serving: 46 | Prep: | Cook: 30mins | Ready in:

Ingredients

- 1 cup chopped zucchini
- 1 cup chopped tomato
- 1/2 cup onion
- 1/3 cup parmesan cheese
- 1/2 cup cheddar cheese
- 1 cup milk
- 2 large eggs, beaten
- 1/2 cup Bisquick
- 1/2 tsp. salt
- 1/8 tsp. pepper
- 1/4 tsp. dried basil, or fresh basil

Direction

- Grease a 9" pie plate.
- Add the first five ingredients and put in pie plate
- Combine the remaining ingredients and pour over the vegetable mixture.
- Bake at 400* until a knife inserted in the center comes out clean, about 30 min.

219. Super Bomb Zucchini Quiche Recipe

Serving: 8 | Prep: | Cook: 1mins | Ready in:

Ingredients

- -6 cups of grated or fine chopped skinless zucchini.
- -1 cup of fresh chopped basil
- -1 cup of fresh chopped parsley
- -1.5 cups shredded sharp chedder cheese
- -1.5 cups of Bisquick or similar
- -1/3 cup of Veg oil
- -1 cup of authentic Italian FINE grated romano cheese
- -6 eggs
- -1 Tsp of garlic powder or granulated garlic (not salt)
- -Season with salt/pep sprinkle if desired

Direction

- Mix Zucchini, basil, parsley & cheddar in one bowl.
- In a separate bowl combine the Bisquick, oil, Romano, 6 eggs & garlic powder and salt &

pep to taste. Beat this mixture very well fully incorporating all.

- Pour this egg mix over Zucchini mixture in the separate bowl, then fold everything together
- Fully. Don't over stir, but do fold in well.
- Grease, spray or butter a 9x13" or similar size square baking pan (Around 2" deep) if you want to serve square pieces, or grease a round pie pan type if you want to serve pie type wedges.
- Pour mix into greased pan evenly, smooth out top.
- Bake at 360-375 degrees for one hour. Oven temps may vary.
- Check often after 40 minutes.
- Let cool fully before cutting!!
- This is made to serve room temp.
- Enjoy!
- Thank Nana!

220. Sweet Onion Gruyere And Bacon Quiche Recipe

Serving: 8 | Prep: | Cook: 40mins | Ready in:

Ingredients

- 6 slices turkey bacon
- 1 cup chopped sweet onion
- 2 tbsp olive oil
- 2 large eggs
- 2 large egg whites (I use egg beaters)
- 3/4 cup evaporated skim milk
- 3/4 cup skim milk
- 2 tsp cornstarch
- 1/2 tsp ground black pepper
- 1/4 tsp salt
- 1/4 tsp nutmeg
- 3/4 cup grated gruyere cheese (I use swiss a lot)
- 1 frozen deep dish 9 inch pie shell

Direction

- Preheat oven to 425 degrees
- In microwave or on stovetop, cook bacon until crisp. Crumble and set aside.
- In a large skillet, heat the oil over medium heat. Add onion and cook until soft (about 10 minutes). Stir in bacon and set aside to cool.
- In mixing bowl, whisk together the eggs and whites. Add evaporated milk, skim milk cornstarch pepper, salt and nutmeg. Then whisk to combine.
- Mix cheese into cooled onion bacon mixture, then spoon the mixture into the pie shell in an even layer. Pour the egg mixture evenly on top.
- Bake the quiche for 30 to 40 minutes, or until golden brown on top and set in the centre. Transfer to a wire rack to cook for 10 minutes before slicing.

221. Swiss Cheese And Mushroom Quiche Recipe

Serving: 4 | Prep: | Cook: 60mins | Ready in:

Ingredients

- 1 10" pie crust
- 1 tsp. margarine
- 1 1/2 cups chopped onion
- 1/4 lb. mushrooms, sliced
- 1/2 tsp. salt
- fresh ground pepper
- a pinch of thyme
- 1/2 tsp. dry mustard
- 2 whole eggs plus 2 egg whites
- 1 1/2 cups milk
- 2 tbsp. flour
- 1 1/2 cups packed grated swiss cheese
- paprika

Direction

- Preheat oven to 375 Degrees.
- Melt the margarine in a small pan. Add onions, and sauté over medium heat for a few

minutes. When they begin to soften, add mushrooms, salt, pepper, thyme, and mustard. Sauté about 5 minutes more and remove from heat.

- Combine eggs, milk and flour and beat well.
- Spread the grated cheese over the bottom of the unbaked crust, and spread the onion-mushroom mixture on top. Pour in the egg mixture and garnish with paprika.
- Bake for 35-45 minutes, or until solid in the center. Serve hot.

222. Swiss Cheese And Smoked Salmon Quiche Recipe

Serving: 8 | Prep: | Cook: 45mins | Ready in:

Ingredients

- 1 cup smoked salmon
- 1/2 cup mayonnaise
- 1/2 cup milk
- 2 eggs
- 1 tablespoon cornstarch
- 1 1/2 cups swiss cheese grated
- 1/3 cup green onions finely chopped
- 1/3 cup celery
- 1/4 teaspoon white pepper
- 1/4 teaspoon paprika
- 9 inch pastry shell

Direction

- Blend mayonnaise, milk, eggs and cornstarch then stir in salmon, cheese, onions and pepper.
- Pour into 9" pastry shall and bake at 350 for 35 minutes.

223. TRISHS QUICHE LORRAINE Recipe

Serving: 48 | Prep: | Cook: 35mins | Ready in:

Ingredients

- 2 deep dish pie shells
- 9 eggs
- 1 c chop deli ham (finely chopped)
- 1/2 c cooked crisp bacon (crumbled)
- 1/2 c chopped fresh baby spinich
- 2 c colby/monterey jack cheese (finely shredded kind)
- 1 c bella sliced mushsrooms (finely chopped)
- 2 tbsp green onion (tops and chive) finely chopped
- 1 small heavy whipped cream
- 1 c half and half
- 2 tsp nutmeg
- 1/2 tsp each salt and pepper

Direction

- Preheat oven to 400.
- Pierce sides and bottom of crusts with fork.
- Place on cookie sheet.
- Cook at 400 for 10 minutes set aside leaving on cookie sheet.
- Cook bacon till crisp. Crumble place 1/2 in each pie crust.
- Place 1/2 of cheese on top of bacon in each pie crust.
- In large bowl mix: all other ingredients, accept leave 1/2 nutmeg for top of pies.
- Blend all ingredients with whisk till completely blended. Pour 1/2 mixture on each pie crust. Top with remaining nutmeg.
- Bake at 325 for 30-40 minutes (keep on cookie sheet) or until knife poked in center comes out clean.
- Let set for 10 minutes before serving.
- Serve with canned or fresh fruit and a lettuce salad.

224. TUSCAN TOMATO PESTO QUICHE Recipe

Serving: 6 | Prep: | Cook: 45mins | Ready in:

Ingredients

- 15 cherry tomatoes
- 1 1/2 cups ricotta cheese
- 1/3 cup sour cream
- 1/3 cup goat cheese softened
- 1/2 cup finely grated parmesan cheese
- 1/3 cup fresh minced basil
- 1 egg
- 2 egg yolks
- salt and pepper to taste
- pastry shell
- 1/3 cup pesto

Direction

- Cut each tomato in half and squeeze out juices. Mix the cheeses, eggs and salt and pepper. Transfer the mixture to the pre-baked pastry shell. Arrange the tomatoes cut side up in the egg mixture and bake in a 425 degree oven for 45 minutes. Remove to cool and fill each tomato piece with prepared pesto.

225. Taco Quiche With Avocado Salsa Recipe

Serving: 8 | Prep: | Cook: 45mins |Ready in:

Ingredients

- 1 ready to bake pastry shell, large and deep dish
- 1 tablespoon oil
- 1/4 cup chopped onion
- 1 large clove garlic, minced
- 1/2 pound lean ground beef
- 2 teaspoons chili powder
- 1/2 teaspoon dried oregano
- 1/2 teaspoon salt   (divided)
- 1/8 teaspoon cayenne pepper
- 1 tablespoon ketchup
- Dash Tabasco
- 3 eggs, slightly beaten
- 1-1/2 cups half and half

- 1 small can green chilies
- 1-1/2 cups shredded mild cheddar cheese
- 1 cup shredded monterey jack cheese
- salsa
- 1 avocado, peeled and diced
- 1 clove garlic, minced
- 1 tablespoon lime juice
- 2 green onions, chopped fine
- 1 medium tomato or 2-3 roma tomatoes, chopped

Direction

- Bake pastry shell for 7 minutes at 400 degrees.
- In skillet, heat oil and sauté' onion and garlic until soft.
- Stir in the ground beef, chili powder, oregano, *1/4* teaspoon salt, cayenne pepper, ketchup and Tabasco sauce.
- Brown the meat mixture, drain well.
- Spoon into baked pie shell.
- In bowl, beat eggs, mix with half and half, *1/4* teaspoon salt, chilies and cheeses.
- Pour mixture over meat.
- Bake at 400 degrees for 40 minutes until center is set and a knife comes out clean.
- Let rest about 15 minutes before serving.
- SALSA
- In bowl, combine all listed ingredients.
- Top with salsa before serving.

226. Tasty Tomato And Zucchini Quiche Recipe

Serving: 8 | Prep: | Cook: 40mins |Ready in:

Ingredients

- tomato and zucchini Quiche (Inspired by the Basic Quiche Recipe from Real Simple Magazine)
- Yields: 2 Complete Quiche and 8 Large and Tasty Servings
- 1 tablespoon olive oil

- 1 large onion, diced
- 4 tomatoes, sliced, lightly salted and patted dry
- 2 medium zucchinis, sliced
- 1/2 pint grape tomatoes, sliced in half
- 3/4 teaspoon kosher salt
- 1/2 teaspoon black pepper
- 1/2 cup fresh flat-leaf parsley, chopped
- 1/2 cup fresh basil, chopped
- 4 eggs
- 3/4 cup half-and-half
- 8 ounces Gruyère, grated
- 1/8 teaspoon ground nutmeg
- 2 store-bought frozen piecrust in tins

Direction

- Heat oven to 375° F.
- In a large skillet, over medium heat, heat the oil. Add the onion, zucchini, 1/2 teaspoon of the salt, and 1/4 teaspoon of the pepper. Cover and cook until the onions and zucchini are softened, 5 to 7 minutes.
- Meanwhile, whisk together the eggs and half-and-half. Stir in the Gruyère, herbs, nutmeg, the remaining salt and pepper, and the onion and zucchini mixture.
- Place the pie crusts on a foil-lined baking sheet. Scrape the egg mixture into the pie crusts; they will be very full. Top with sliced grape tomatoes. Bake until the filling is set and a knife inserted into the center comes out clean, about 40 minutes. Let rest for 5 minutes. Cut into wedges and serve.

227.   Tearoom Quiche Recipe

Serving: 6 | Prep: | Cook: 60mins | Ready in:

Ingredients

- 8 eggs
- 1 tablespoon dried chives
- 1 teaspoon salt
- 3 or 4 cups shredded cheese, any variety

- 8-ounce carton sour cream
- 1 teaspoon dry mustard
- 1/2 teaspoon pepper
- 2 cups broccoli, chopped, steamed and drained

Direction

- Preheat oven to 350 degrees.
- Beat eggs; add sour cream and spices, mixing well.
- Stir in broccoli and add as much cheese as can be blended with other ingredients.
- Pour into an ungreased glass quiche dish and bake at 350 degrees for one hour or until firm in the center.

228.   The No Treadmill Required Quiche Recipe

Serving: 23 | Prep: | Cook: 60mins | Ready in:

Ingredients

- 8 eggs- I used Jumbo doesn't matter...
- 1 tsp. salt
- 1 tsp. black pepper
- 1 handful of mushrooms
- 1/2 green or red pepper
- 1/4 cup of onion
- 1 cup milk- I use 2%
- 3/4 cup shredded sharp cheddar or American cheese
- 1 tbsp. of margarine
- dash of parsley
- 1 square or round like 9x9 or close too, pyrex glass dish worked good for me and didn't stick at all....

Direction

- Start by dicing the veggies and then put in container and microwave for about a minute to get them tender.

- Crack the eggs in another bowl and add the salt, pepper, milk, parsley and whisk well.
- After the veggies cooled down add them to eggs and the margarine and half the cheese.
- Spray a little cooking spray in the dish and add the egg mixture.
- Place dish on the lower rack of the oven on a cookie sheet in a 325 degree oven for about 60-70 minutes.
- 20 minutes prior to doneness add the remaining cheese on top.
- After that let it cool for a second then indulge into the greatest no crust, no guilt, healthy treat you will love.

229. Three Cheese And Tomato Quiche Recipe

Serving: 8 | Prep: | Cook: 30mins | Ready in:

Ingredients

- 1 pie crust (9 inch), blind bake
- 1 ounce parmesan cheese, fresh shredded
- 2 ounces mozzarella cheese, shredded
- 2 ounces swiss cheese, shredded
- 4 green onions, sliced
- 1 egg
- 1 egg yolk
- 1 cup whipping cream
- salt and pepper, to taste
- 2 dashes nutmeg
- 1 tablespoon olive oil
- 3 ripe tomatoes, medium, sliced 1/4" thick
- 2 teaspoons Dijon mustard
- 1 teaspoon dried oregano (or 2 teaspoons chopped fresh)
- 1 teaspoon dried basil (or 8 leaves freshly chopped basil)

Direction

- Heat oven to 375.

- In food processor container, add egg, egg yolk, cream, salt, pepper and nutmeg. Process to mix.
- In oil, sauté green onions until wilted; remove. Add tomato slices to skillet and cook over medium heat until skin loosens. Transfer to paper towels and lift off skins. Pat off moisture.
- Brush mustard onto bottom of cooled crust. Add mozzarella in an even layer. Place tomato slices, green onions, oregano and basil over mozzarella. Salt & pepper lightly. Top with Swiss. Slowly pour in egg mixture. Sprinkle with parmesan cheese.
- Bake 25 to 30 minutes or until puffy and browned. Cool on rack to lukewarm. Serve at room temperature.
- NOTE: Use a gluten-free pie crust to make this gluten-free.

230. Tofu Bobotie Recipe

Serving: 4 | Prep: | Cook: 60mins | Ready in:

Ingredients

- 1/4 cup raisins
- 1/4 onion, chopped fine
- 1/2 tbsp. vegetable oil
- 1/2 tbsp. ginger, minced
- 1/2 tbsp. garlic, minced
- 1 tbsp. curry powder
- 1/8 cup cider vinegar
- 1 tbsp. apricot jam
- 1 1/2 tbsp. brown sugar
- 1/8 cup slivered almonds, toasted
- 1 500g pkg. firm tofu, frozen overnight, then defrosted and squeezed to release excess water, then crumbled.
- 3 slices whole wheat bread, diced into about 1/2 inch squares
- 1 19oz./540 ml. can coconut milk, divided in two
- salt and pepper, to taste

- 2 whole eggs
- 1 banana, sliced lengthwise into strips

Direction

- Soak raisins in warm water and set aside.
- Sauté onion in oil for 1-2 minutes, add ginger, garlic and curry powder and sauté a minute longer. Add vinegar, jam and brown sugar and sauté to blend, about 2 minutes. Add almonds.
- Add plumped and drained raisins, then crumbled tofu and cook 5 minutes, stirring to blend. Transfer mixture to a bowl and set aside.
- Soak diced bread cubes in 1/2 can of coconut milk, then mix into tofu mixture. Season to taste with salt and pepper.
- To assemble bobotie, grease a 9" oven proof glass pie or cake pan and press mixture to fill. Can prepare to this point one day in advance, and keep covered and refrigerated.
- Preheat oven to 350F.
- Beat remaining 1/2 can coconut milk with two eggs. Place banana slices on top of bobotie and cover with milk mixture. Bake in oven for 35 minutes or until set.

231. Tomato And Goat Cheese Quiche Recipe

Serving: 4 | Prep: | Cook: 40mins | Ready in:

Ingredients

- 3/4 cup whipping cream
- 2 eggs
- salt and pepper to taste
- 3/4 cup shredded swiss cheese
- 1/2 cup shredded mozzarella cheese
- 1/4 cup soft goat cheese
- 3 roma tomatoes, seeded and slced.
- 1/4 cup cream cheese
- 1/8 teaspoon minced garlic
- 2 Tbl chives

- Pre-baked pie crust or pastry for (9-inch) tart

Direction

- Whisk together whipping cream, eggs and dash each salt and pepper.
- Combine shredded Swiss and mozzarella cheeses in small bowl. In another bowl, beat goat cheese, cream cheese, garlic, chives, 1/2 teaspoon salt and pepper to taste until smooth.
- Scatter shredded cheeses over bottom of pastry. Layer tomatoes over shredded cheese. Spoon goat cheese mixture in small dollops over top. Slowly pour egg mixture over all.
- Place tart pan on baking sheet to make handling easier and catch any overflow. Bake at 375 degrees until top is lightly browned, about 35 to 40 minutes. Set aside 10 minutes before cutting. Serve warm or at room temperature.

232. Tomato Basil Quiche Recipe

Serving: 6 | Prep: | Cook: 45mins | Ready in:

Ingredients

- crust for 10-inch quiche pan
- 1 teaspoon olive oil
- 1 cup slivered onion -sweet onion texas or vidilla
- 1 clove garlic, chopped-2 if you love it like i do.
- 3/4 cup shredded mozzarella cheese - i like to get the smoked mozzarella but any will do.
- 1 cup 1/4-inch-thick slices plum tomato
- 1/4 cup shredded fresh basil
- 1 cup evaporated skim milk
- 1-1/2 teaspoons cornstarch
- 1/4 teaspoon black pepper
- 2 eggs
- 1 egg white

Direction

- Preheat oven to 350 degrees. Line 10-inch quiche pan with crust. Heat non-stick pan with olive oil; sauté onion and garlic until slightly brown. Spread onion mixture on crust and sprinkle cheese on top. Arrange tomato slices over cheese. Top with basil.
- Combine milk, cornstarch, pepper, and eggs. Process in blender until smooth. Carefully pour over tomatoes. Bake 45 minutes or until a knife inserted near the center comes out clean. Let stand 10 minutes before serving. You can also use sun dried tomato for a little different taste sometimes I add bacon or pancetta and they mix in well also.

- Spread 1 C. shredded cheese in the bottom of pie crust.
- Layer onions over cheese, and top with tomatoes.
- Cover with egg mixture.
- Sprinkle top with remaining 1/2 C. shredded cheese.
- Bake in preheated oven for 10 minutes.
- Reduce heat to 350 degrees and bake for 15-20 minutes, or until filling is puffed and golden brown.
- Serve warm.
- -Susana

233. Tomato Quiche Recipe

Serving: 8 | Prep: | Cook: 45mins | Ready in:

Ingredients

- 1 Tbs. olive oil
- 1 onion, sliced
- 2 tomatoes, peeled and sliced
- 2 Tbs. all-purpose flour
- 2 tsp. dried basil
- 3 eggs, beaten
- 1/2 C. milk
- 1/2 tsp. salt and pepper to taste
- 1 9-inch unbaked deep dish pie crust
- 1 1/2 C. shredded colby-monterey jack cheese, divided

Direction

- Directions
- Preheat oven to 400 degrees.
- Bake pie shell in preheated oven for 8 minutes.
- Meanwhile, heat olive oil in a large skillet over medium heat.
- Sauté onion until soft; remove from skillet.
- Sprinkle tomato slices with flour and basil, then sauté 1 minute on each side.
- In a small bowl, whisk together eggs and milk.
- Season with salt and pepper.

234. Vegan Hokkaido And Rosemary Quiche Recipe

Serving: 8 | Prep: | Cook: 1hours50mins | Ready in:

Ingredients

- 500g hokkaido pumpkin (peeled and seeded)
- 100g seitan
- 1 courgette
- 1 carrot
- 1 shallot
- 2 tbsp olive oil
- salt (just taste the filling to see how much you need)
- a few splashes of soya sauce
- a bit of water
- rosemary
- marjoram
- a few pinches of powdered veg bouillon

Direction

- 1. Start by preparing the dough, sift your flour and salt in a large bowl.
- 2. Add the oil, water and mix with a fork to get rid of lumps.
- 3. Then work it with your hands for a bit and shape it into a ball.

- 4. On a floured surface stretch the dough with a rolling pin and then lay it in a cake tin of about 28cm.
- 5. For the filling, peel and seed the pumpkin, cut it into small chunks and do the same with the other veggies (apart from the courgette that I don't peel).
- 6. Heat up a frying pan, add the olive oil, carrot and shallot.
- 7. Let them sweat a bit and then add the rest of the cut up veggies, the seitan, a few splashes of soya sauce, the veg bouillon, the rosemary and marjoram.
- 8. Add some water once you see they start getting a bit dry, this will help them stay soft and prevent them from sticking to the bottom of the pan.
- 9. Blend everything and add more salt if needed as the pumpkin will make the filling very sweet.
- 10. Smooth the filling on the dough, then bake for about 40 mins in a preheated oven at 200C.
- 11. Make sure you allow it to cool down for a few hours before eating it.

---

235. Vegan Quiche Recipe

Serving: 0 | Prep: | Cook: 80mins | Ready in:

Ingredients

- Dough:
- 250g plain flour
- 120ml water
- 60ml olive oil
- 1/2 tsp salt
- Filling:
- 400g tofu
- about 120ml unsweetened soya milk
- 2 stalks of celery
- 1 carrot
- 1 onion
- 1 courgette
- 4 tbsp nutritional yeast
- 2 tbsp tahini
- 2 tbsp olive oil
- a pinch of paprika and turmeric
- a few splashes of soya sauce
- a pinch of salt

Direction

- 1. Start by making the dough so sift the flour and salt in a large bowl, mix well.
- 2. Then add the olive oil, water and with a fork combine everything together.
- 3. Knead well with your hands and make a ball of it.
- 4. On a floured surface flatten it out with a rolling pin and place it in a baking tin of about 28cm.
- 5. For the filling, cut in very small pieces your veggies (onion, celery, carrot and courgette).
- 6. Add the oil to a preheated frying pan and sauté them until almost soft adding the salt halfway through.
- 7. In a separate bowl/glass blend the tofu, nutritional yeast, tahini, soya milk, soya sauce, and spices until smooth.
- 8. One the veggies are soft add them to the tofu mixture.
- 9. Fill the dough making sure it's even and bake for about 35/40 mins at 200C in a preheated oven.

---

236. Vegetable Frittita Recipe

Serving: 0 | Prep: | Cook: 20mins | Ready in:

Ingredients

- 6 eggs
- 3 tbsp milk
- fresh mushrooms sliced
- fresh broccoli, Small head cut up
- 1 small onion chopped
- chives chopped (or 2 tbsp dried)
- 1 bell pepper chopped
- 1/2 pint grape or cherry tomatoes sliced

- 1 cup spinach leaves
- 1/4 cup parmesan cheese
- 1 cup shredded cheese
- salt & pepper to taste
- 1 tsp garlic powder
- butter

Direction

- Preheat oven to 350.
- Chop all veggies above (or your choice) and set aside.
- Beat eggs with milk & cheeses.
- In large skillet (need to be able to put in oven), melt 3 tbsp. butter.
- Add veggies and sauté till tender.
- Pour egg mixture over.
- Put in oven and bake till set and cooked about 15-20 minutes.

237.   Vegetable Pie Recipe

Serving: 0 | Prep: | Cook: 45mins | Ready in:

Ingredients

- 2 c chopped brocolli or cauliflower
- 1/3 c chopped onion
- 1/3 c chopped pepper ,red green or yellow
- 1 c shredded old cheddar....i used a mixture of cheddar and baby parmesan
- 1/2 c Bisquick or homemade baking mix
- 1 c milk
- 1/2 tsp eack salt and pepper
- 2 eggs
- pinch cayenne

Direction

- *The above recipe is a basic and to that I added asparagus, cilantro and 1 tablespoon shelled hemp seed.
- Spray a pie plate with pam. Mix together the first 4 ingredients. Mix the Bisquick, (will post Bisquick substitute recipe) milk, hemp seed,

cayenne, salt and pepper and eggs. Blend well and pour over the veggies and cheese.
- I laid asparagus on top in a spoke design.
- Cook 35 - 45 mins till brown and toothpick inserted comes out clean.

238.   Vegetable Quiche Recipe

Serving: 4 | Prep: | Cook: 35mins | Ready in:

Ingredients

- 2 cups lightly cooked broccoli, cut into bite-sized pieces
- 1/2 c chopped onion
- 1/2 red sweet pepper, cut into bite-sized pieces
- 1 1/3 c milk
- 1 1/3 c shredded cheese (I use a 4-cheese mix)
- 2/3 c biscuit mix (e.g., Bisquick)
- 4 eggs
- salt and pepper to taste.

Direction

- Grease pie plate or quiche dish. Place broccoli, onion, red pepper and cheese in dish.
- In a blender, mix together milk, biscuit mix, eggs, salt and pepper. Mix well. Pour over vegetables in dish.
- Bake at 375F for 30 minutes. Allow to set for 5 minutes before serving.

239.   Vegetarian Mini Quiche Recipe

Serving: 6 | Prep: | Cook: 30mins | Ready in:

Ingredients

- 2 table spoons of chick peas (i used canned but you can soak your own)

- 2 table spoons of green lentels (canned but you can soak your own)
- 1 large onion
- 6 small tomatoes
- 12 slices of whole meal bread
- 12 table spoons of light tasty cheese
- 2 large eggs
- 1 table spoon of milk
- salt and pepper to taste
- min of a 12 muffin tray
- Greased baking tray
- Large Sauce pan

Direction

- Pre heat oven to 180*c.
- Cut the tomatoes in half and lay onto the greased tray. Cook for 1/2 an hour, or until can be easily skinned.
- Remove skins and put the tomatoes into a large bowl. Drain onto a piece of kitchen towel. (I use my fingers for the next step but you can use a blender or a masher.)
- Squish up the tomato into smallish pieces.
- Add your chick peas and lentils and stir together.
- Finely dice the onion and cook in your large pan until clear.
- Add your tomato mix and stir through. Cook until hot through.
- Leave that to cool.
- Beat your eggs and add the milk.
- Cut the crusts off your bread and roll flat with a rolling pin.
- Put the bread into your muffin tray and brush with some milk.
- Bake the bread in the muffin tray in the oven while your tomato mix cools. (7mins)
- Evenly spoon tomato mix into your bread and top each with a table spoon of cheese.
- Cook in the oven until the egg has set and the cheese has melted. This should take around 30 mins.
- ENJOY!

240.   Vegetarian Quiche Recipe

Serving: 68 | Prep: | Cook: 40mins | Ready in:

Ingredients

- Pastry
- Half kilo flour
- 250 gr of good butter straight from fridge
- 2.5 tbl oilive oil
- Half glass ice cold water
- Quiche filling
- Glass of natural yogurt
- 2 X glass of grated mature cheese
- 3 eggs
- 200 ml of milk
- tsp ground nutmeg
- salt pepper
- variety of diced vegetables of your liking, par boiled/roasted or stir fried as desired (carrots, spinach,parnsips, cauliflower, mushrooms, onion, garlic

Direction

- To make the pastry combine all of the ingredients and with a knife break up the butter. Add ice cold water quickly to get it into a compact ball without being too fussy in ensuring all the butter is rubbed in properly. NB-water has to be very cold when adding to bind. Speed and efficiency is key here. Once you have a block of pastry -leave to sit in a fridge for min two hours.
- Remove and grease a baking tray or dish-roll out the pastry so that it is even and not too thick. Few mil is good.
- To make the filling simply whisk together all the ingredients except the vegetables/one cup of cheese until fluffy. Add the par cooked veg to the pastry lined tray and then add in the quiche mixture. Sprinkle over the last cup of cheese, salt and pepper.
- Pre heat oven to 180 deg C and let it cook here for 40 mins or until browning.

241. Veggie Wonton Quiches Recipe

Serving: 24 | Prep: | Cook: 30mins | Ready in:

Ingredients

- 24 wonton wrappers
- 1 cup finely chopped fresh broccoli, I am going to use snow peas
- 3/4 cup diced fresh mushrooms
- 1/2 diced sweet red pepper
- 1/4 cup finly chopped onion, we are using more
- 2 teaspoons vegetable oil
- 3 eggs
- 1 tablespoon water
- 2 teaspoons dried parsley flakes, or fesh chopped very fine
- 1/4 teaspoon salt, we are using sea salt
- 1/4 teaspoon dried thyme, or finely chopped fresh
- 1/4 teaspoon pepper
- dash of cayenne pepper
- 3/4 cup shredded cheddar cheese

Direction

- Gently press wonton wrappers into miniature muffin cups coated with non-stick cooking spray.
- Lightly coat wontons with non-stick cooking spray.
- Bake at 350 f degrees for five minutes.
- Remove wontons from cups, place upside down on baking sheets.
- Lightly coat the bottom and sides of the wontons with non-stick spray.
- Bake five minutes longer or until light golden brown.
- These can be prepared ahead.
- Meanwhile, in a non-stick, cook the broccoli, mushrooms, red pepper and onion in oil over medium heat for four to five minutes or until crisp-tender,
- In a bowl, whisk eggs and water; stir in seasonings.
- Add to vegetable mixture, cook over medium heat until egg is completely set, about four minutes.
- Remove from heat and stir in the cheese.
- Spoon about 1 tablespoon of the mixture into each wonton cup.
- Bake for five minutes, or until filling is heated through.
- Serve warm.

242. West Coast Smoked Salmon And Cream Cheese Quiche Recipe

Serving: 8 | Prep: | Cook: 45mins | Ready in:

Ingredients

- 6 ounces smoked salmon
- 4 ounces cream cheese
- 1 cup shredded swiss cheese
- 1/2-cup grated asiago cheese
- 3 eggs
- 1-1/2 cups light cream
- 1/2-teaspoon kosher salt
- 1/4-teaspoon freshly ground black pepper
- 2 tablespoons fresh dill chopped
- Parmesan Crust:
- 2 cups all purpose flour
- 3/4 teaspoon kosher salt
- 1/2 cup cold unsalted butter cut into small bits
- 1/2 cup grated parmesan cheese
- 1/3 cup ice water

Direction

- Heat oven to 425.
- To make crust combine flour and salt in a food processor or mixing bowl.
- Add butter and process or combine with a fork until small particles are formed.

- Add grated parmesan cheese and process briefly to combine.
- If using a food processor transfer contents to a mixing bowl.
- Add cold water and mix to make a ball of dough.
- Sprinkle about 3 tablespoons flour on a board and roll the dough into a 12" circle. Transfer dough to 10" tart pan or quiche pan.
- Lay a piece of foil inside and put dried beans inside the foil.
- This keeps the crust from puffing up when it bakes then bake crust 8 minutes.
- Remove foil and beans and bake 3 minutes longer.
- Remove from oven and allow to cool while making filling.
- Reduce oven temperature to 350.
- For filling spread crumbled smoked salmon over crust.
- Cut cream cheese into bits and scatter over salmon.
- Sprinkle with Swiss cheese and Asiago cheese.
- Beat eggs in a mixing bowl then add cream, salt, pepper and dill then pour into crust.
- Bake quiche until golden brown and puffed then let stand 15 minutes before serving.

---

243. Wild Rice And Ham Quiche Recipe

Serving: 6 | Prep: | Cook: 45mins | Ready in:

Ingredients

- 1 ready made pie crust
- Filling
- 1 cup cooked ham, cubed
- 1/2 cup wild rice, cooked
- 1/3 cup red pepper, finely chopped
- 1/4 cup scallion, thinly sliced
- 1 4.5 oz. jar mushrooms, sliced and well drained
- custard

- 3 eggs
- 1 cup sour cream
- 1 tbls. Dijon mustard
- salt and pepper to taste
- Topping
- 2 cups swiss cheese, grated

Direction

- Preheat oven to 425.
- Using a 9 inch pie pan, press crust into bottom and up sides of pan.
- DO NOT DOCK CRUST.
- Bake for 10-12 minutes.
- Remove from oven and lower heat to 400.
- In mixing bowl, add all filling ingredients and mix well.
- In another mixing bowl, add eggs and beat until blended.
- Add remaining custard ingredients and mix well.
- Sprinkle 1 cup of Swiss cheese over bottom of cooled crust.
- Spread filling mixture over cheese.
- Pour custard mixture over filling.
- Sprinkle with remaining Swiss cheese.
- Bake for 30-35 minutes.
- Let sit for 10 minutes before serving.

---

244. Zesty Quiche Monterey Recipe

Serving: 8 | Prep: | Cook: 45mins | Ready in:

Ingredients

- 1 Pillsbury® Refrigerated pie crust
- 1 lb bacon, diced and cooked, reserve fat for other uses
- 6 eggs
- 1 1/2 cups heavy cream
- Pinch of salt
- Pinch of nutmeg
- Pinch of cayenne

- 1 1/2 cups shredded monterey jack cheese
- 2 mild banana peppers, seeded and chopped
- 2 cups fresh ruby chard (leaves and stems), chopped and packed

Direction

- Line a 10-inch pie plate with the crust and bake per package directions for an unbaked filling. Allow to cool while preparing the filling.
- In a medium mixing bowl, whisk the eggs, heavy cream, and seasonings.
- In another large bowl, toss the peppers, chard, shredded cheese and bacon, to evenly mix.
- Spoon the veggie/bacon mixture into the cooled pie crust. Pour the blended cream and eggs over.
- Since the pastry has already been baked, cover the crust rim with strips of aluminum foil to prevent over-browning.
- Bake the quiche in a preheated 375F deg oven for 35 to 45 minutes, or until the custard is set and the surface is lightly browned.
- Serve with crispy hash browns and fresh sliced tomatoes.

245. Zucchini Bacon Quiche Recipe

Serving: 6 | Prep: | Cook: 40mins | Ready in:

Ingredients

- 1 1/4 cups of all purpose flour
- 2 teaspoons of baking powder
- 1/2 tsp of salt
- 1/2 tsp of basil
- 1/2 cup of unsalted butter, room temperature
- 1/2 cup of sour cream
- Filling:
- 6 strips of bacon, diced
- 3 cups of thinly sliced zucchini
- 1 medium onion chopped
- 1 clove of garlic, chopped

- 2 eggs beaten
- 1/4 tsp of dried basil
- 1/4 tsp of dried oregano
- 2 cups of shredded mozzarella cheese
- 2 tablespoons of chopped fresh parsley
- 1/2 tsp of pepper
- generous pinch of salt

Direction

- In a bowl, combine the flour, baking powder, salt and basil.
- Cut in the butter using a pastry cutter until the flour mixture is crumbly.
- Add sour cream, knead and roll into a ball.
- Wrap in plastic wrap and chill for at least 30 minutes.
- Press the dough into a 9 inch pie pan.
- Bake at 375 degrees for 10 minutes.
- Cool completely.
- Cook the bacon in a skillet over medium heat until crisp.
- Remove and drain on paper towel.
- Using two tablespoons of the bacon drippings, sauté the prepped zucchini, onion, and garlic until tender.
- In a large bowl, combine eggs, cheese seasonings, bacon and zucchini mixture.
- Pour into baked cooled crust.
- Bake at 375 degrees for 20 minutes or until a knife inserted in the center comes out clean. Cover the edges of the pastry with foil if it starts to brown too quickly.

246. Zucchini Cashew Quiche Recipe

Serving: 6 | Prep: | Cook: 45mins | Ready in:

Ingredients

- 1-8 roll can crescent-style rolls (I used reduced fat)
- 3/4 cup cashews (you may wish to chop up slightly in your f.p.)

- 3 medium zuchinni
- 3 T butter or margarine, or your favorite EVOO for sauteeing
- 1/4 t garlic powder, or use minced garlic-in-a-jar like I do
- 1/4 t salt
- 1/8 t pepper
- 6 oz chunk Monterey Jack (reduced fat) cheese or whatever cheese you have on hand or use pre-shredded to save on time
- 2 eggs
- 1 c milk (I always use skim and it works fine)

Direction

- Preheat oven to 325 Degrees F.
- Remove dough from package and tear apart each individual roll. Line 9 inch deep dish pie plate with same, by placing points of the triangle in the center; pat dough together at seams to seal and smooth. (Get as fancy with the edge as you want, LOL!)
- Sprinkle bottom of crust with the cashews (slightly chopped if you wish)
- Medium slice the zucchini (use the F.P.! lots less work!)
- Melt butter or margarine or use your EVOO in a large skillet and sauté the zucchini until crisp-tender. Add garlic, salt and pepper and toss.
- Spoon zucchini over cashews in the pie plate.
- Process your cheese into 1/8 inch pieces if you have a chunk (skip this if you are using pre-shredded) and set aside.
- Combine eggs and milk in the F.P. (food processor) and mix well.
- Pour milk/egg mixture over top of zucchini.
- Sprinkle cheese on top.
- Bake for 45 minutes until set. (I use my trusty cake tester or you can also use a toothpick).
- Enjoy with a crisp green salad!

247. Zucchini Panko Pie Recipe

Serving: 0 | Prep: | Cook: 35mins | Ready in:

Ingredients

- Base:
- cooking oil spray- or butter or olive oil
- 1/2 cup panko breadcrumbs
- Filling:
- 4 eggs beaten
- zest of one lemon
- 1 Tbs lemon juice
- 1/4 cup grated cheese (recipe called for Parmesan I used Asagio)
- 1/4 cup panko breakcrumbs
- 1/2 tsp salt
- 1/4 tsp pepper
- 1/2 tsp herbs De Provance (my addition)
- 1 medium zucchini grated
- 2 Tbs grated onion (my addition)
- 1 medium zucchini thinly sliced
- Topping:
- 1/2 cup panko breadcrumbs
- 1/4 cup grated parmesan cheese (I used Asagio)

Direction

- Coat (or butter my suggestion) a 9 inch pie pan with cooking spray.
- Sprinkle on the breadcrumbs
- Mix the beaten eggs together with lemon zest, lemon juice, salt and pepper, 1/4 cup Panko, 1/4 cup grated cheese and stir to combine
- Now place a thin layer on the sliced zucchini over the breadcrumbs in the pan
- Pour on 1/3 cup of egg zucchini mixture, more sliced zucchini and repeat layers finishing with sliced zucchini on top
- Sprinkle on the Panko and grated cheese as the last topping
- Bake in a preheated 350 F oven about 35 minutes or top is lightly browned
- Cool 10 minutes in the pan, and slice and serve.

- Note: I think a dollop of yogurt or sour cream would be nice.

248.   Zuquiche Crustless Zucchini Quiche Recipe

Serving: 12 | Prep: | Cook: 40mins | Ready in:

Ingredients

- 2 cups shredded zucchini
- 1/2 teaspoon salt
- 1 clove garlic, minced
- 2 green onions, diced
- 1/2 cup diced red pepper
- 1/2 cup flour
- 1/2 teaspoon baking powder
- 1/4 teaspoon salt
- 1/4 teaspoon ground black pepper
- one egg, lightly beaten
- 1/2 cup milk
- 2 TBSP melted butter
- 1 cup shredded mozzarella cheese

Direction

- Preheat oven to 375 degrees.
- Spray an 8 X 8 glass baking dish with cooking spray.
- Place shredded zucchini in a medium bowl and sprinkle with 1/2 teaspoon salt.
- Let it sit for about 15 minutes to allow the liquid to separate from the zucchini.
- Then strain/squeeze the zucchini dry. You want it as dry as possible.
- In a large bowl, whisk together flour, baking powder, pepper, and 1/4 tsp. salt.
- In a separate bowl, mix together egg, milk, and butter.
- 8. Stir egg mixture into dry mixture just until blended.
- 9. Fold in veggies and cheese and mix just until incorporated.

- 10. Spread in greased baking dish and bake 30-40 minutes until top is lightly browned and toothpick inserted into center comes out clean.
- 11. Allow to cool about 10 minutes before serving.

249.   Salmone Quiche Recipe

Serving: 6 | Prep: | Cook: 40mins | Ready in:

Ingredients

- pastry for 9-inch pie, unbaked
- 600 grams of smoked salmon
- 1 tablespoons lemon juice
- 1 onion, minced
- 1 1/2 tomatos
- 2 tablespoons butter
- 2 tablespoons chopped fresh parsley
- 6 egg, beaten
- 1 1/2 cups milk
- 1 teaspoon seasoned salt
- dash pepper, white or black
- a cup of cream cheese
- a bowl of spinach
- black olives

Direction

- Bake crust in a 450° oven for 5 minutes. Drain salmon liquid, if there is any, into a cup. Put salmon in a bowl and remove bones and skin, if there is any; flake salmon. Put salmon pastry; sprinkle with lemon juice. Cook onion, tomatoes and the spinach in the butter; transfer to the pie crust and sprinkle with parsley, add the cream cheese
- Mix the salmon liquid with eggs, milk, and seasoned salt and pepper; pour over salmon. Bake quiche at 350° for 45 to 50 minutes, or until firm.
- Serve this salmon quiche hot.

250. Sun Dried Tomato And Zucchini Quiche Recipe

Serving: 8 | Prep: | Cook: 35mins | Ready in:

Ingredients

- store bought pie dough (not sweetened)
- 1 medium brown/ yellow onion
- 1/4 cup drained, chopped sun-dried tomatoes
- 1/3 cup drained, chopped sun-dried zucchini (or eggplant or roasted peppers... create!)
- 1/4 cup shredded fresh basil leaves
- 3/4 cup grated gruyere cheese (authentic is best, but you could get away with the cheap "swiss cheese" version if on a budget)
- 1/4 cup grated parmesan (please be authentic on this one)
- 3 eggs
- 3/4 cup cream (I've learned that it is best to use cream (even if it's a lower-fat verions, who knows how they make that) rather than 1/2 and 1/2 or else the quiche won't rise)
- 1/4 cup tasty cheese (parmesean again or get creative)

Direction

- Thaw dough enough to line pie dish, read directions on package if prebaking is needed for an open-topped savory pie, usually only 10 minutes, if so, line crust with parchment paper and fill with dried beans so that the crust doesn't rise. This is also better than punching holes in the bottom.
- Heat oil from tomatoes in medium sauce pan and sauté onion till soft.
- Spread onion, then tomato, zucchini, basil, gruyere and first part of parmesan into the crust.
- In separate bowl, combine egg and cream, season with salt and pepper to your taste.
- Pour eggs and cream mixture over quiche and sprinkle tasty cheese on top.
- Bake in moderate oven for about 35 minutes or until set (brown atop).

Index

Conclusion

Thank you again for downloading this book!

I hope you enjoyed reading about my book!

If you enjoyed this book, please take the time to share your thoughts and post a review on Amazon. It'd be greatly appreciated!

Write me an honest review about the book – I truly value your opinion and thoughts and I will incorporate them into my next book, which is already underway.

Thank you!

If you have any questions, **feel free to contact at:** *author@bisquerecipes.com*

Mary Yoder

bisquerecipes.com

Printed in Great Britain
by Amazon

54994605R00073